# Herbed-Wine Cuisine

# Herbed-Wine Cuisine

### Creating & Cooking
### with Herb-Infused Wines

Janice Therese Mancuso

*A Storey Publishing Book*

Storey Communications, Inc.
Schoolhouse Road
Pownal, Vermont 05261

*The mission of Storey Communications is to serve our customers by publishing practical information that encourages personal independence in harmony with the environment.*

Edited by Pamela Lappies and Charlotte DuChene
Cover design by Eva Weymouth & Meredith Maker
Cover photographs by Jim Coon
Back cover inset photograph by Paul Rocheleau
Text design by Jonathan Nix
Production by Erin Lincourt
Indexed by Gail Damerow

Printed in the United States by R. R. Donnelley
10 9 8 7 6 5 4 3 2 1

**Library of Congress Cataloging-in-Publication Data**

Mancuso, Janice Therese, [date]
    Herbed-wine cuisine : creating & cooking with herb-infused wines /Janice
    Therese Mancuso
        p.   cm.
    "A Storey Publishing Book"
    Includes index.
    ISBN 0-88266-967-2 (hc : alk. paper)
    1. Cookery (Wine)   2. Cookery (Herbs)   3. Menus.   I. Title.
TX726.M285   1997
641.6'22—dc21
                                                                    97-9076
                                                                    CIP

# Table of Contents

# To Theresa V. Mauro

# Acknowledgments

**M**any thanks to Gloria Marik of Wild Herb Winery in Cary, North Carolina. Our collaboration on my development of recipes for her herbal wines led, in part, to this book.

Special thanks to Barbara King (whose assistance has been invaluable), Tim Johnson, and the employees of Becklyn Publishing Group, Inc., in Cary, North Carolina. Their feedback as taste testers resulted in adjustments to several recipes, such as adding cheese to the Vegetable Pot Pie and serving fruit as a topping with the Rice Custard. A lively discussion with Tim about an "instruction manual on pasta eating" for the Bow-Tie Pasta Salad led to the addition of serving instructions with the recipes.

Thanks also to Dominick Ciccarelli, independent financial consultant, and Gina Miller, of Remax, both in Cary, North Carolina; Doug Andre, president of Junior Achievement, and Donna Naylor, of Moore and Johnson Agency, both in Raleigh, North Carolina; and the other taste testers who made working on this collection of recipes so enjoyable.

A basket of thanks to my family and special friends, who share a love of good food and always offer support and encouragement.

Finally, a bouquet to Gwen Steege, the editor who envisioned this book, diligently answered my questions, and allowed me the opportunity to create these wonderful recipes.

# Introduction

For years, wine has been the secret ingredient in many of the recipes I've prepared. Along with other flavorings and seasonings, wine was added to a list that included a tablespoon of this and a teaspoon of that. While developing recipes, I became intrigued with the idea of flavoring wine. After all, vinegars and oils are offered in a variety of flavors, so why not wine?

My approach to flavoring wines was based on my cooking techniques and favorite foods. Sautéed, baked, and broiled foods are greatly enhanced by marinades and sauces. I started flavoring the wines with the ingredients I used most often — garlic, lemon, basil, oregano, parsley, chives, raspberries, and even roasted red peppers.

Pleased with the results, I became inventive, adding orange and mango to Chardonnay wine, and coriander seeds and peppercorns to Rhine wine. I tried chili peppers and cumin seeds in Pinot Noir, and sun-dried tomatoes and garlic in Merlot. I even added assorted herbs and garlic to rosé. After the wines steeped for a few weeks, it was easy to replace almost any liquid ingredient in a recipe. A flavored wine was substituted for vinegar in a marinade or for chicken stock in a sauce.

What started as a novel approach to cooking with herbal wines has turned into this collection of more than 50 recipes for flavoring wines with herbs, spices, fruits, and vegetables, and more than 120 recipes for using the wines when cooking.

Part One of this book presents the recipes for flavoring wines, offers information on selecting wines and seasonings for creating your own special flavors, and provides gift ideas and packaging suggestions. Part Two contains recipes for dishes from appetizers to desserts, each using a flavored wine from Part One. It also includes information on recipe ingredients, suggestions for adjusting the recipes, and a variety of menus for brunch, lunch, and dinner.

Flavoring wine allows you to create a special blend of ingredients that enhances the food you cook. Not only are they a pleasure to cook with, they are also a pleasure to create.

# Part One

# The Flavored-Wine Recipes

able wines are an excellent addition to cooking. They enhance the food by tenderizing and moisturizing while imparting their subtle flavor. Herbs and spices are the ingredients that personalize a recipe. Think of how bland food would be without seasonings. Different combinations of herbs, spices, and other flavors, and the use of various cooking methods, such as broiling, baking, and sautéing, produce vastly different results, changing the taste, texture, and appearance of any food.

Although flavoring wines is not new — sangria and mulled wine have been around for centuries — cooking with flavored wine is a relatively new approach in preparing food. Flavored wines add an extra dimension to food without requiring the cook to add other seasonings while cooking. It's an easier way of cooking, and healthy, too, since fat and sodium are greatly reduced. 🍇

# Chapter One
## About Wine

*Fill ev'ry glass, for wine inspires us,*
*And fires us*
*With courage, love and joy.*

— John Gay

There are many kinds of wine available on the market, and each has a unique taste, based on the type of grapes and the fermentation process used. The recipes in this section vary from sweet to spicy, using a variety of white, red, and rosé wines.

The following guidelines will give you the basics on choosing wine for flavoring and cooking. Keep in mind that within each varietal, the wines range in taste from sweet to dry and in body from light to heavy. The characteristics of the wine will determine how it will be flavored and how it can be used when cooking.

Another consideration is price. Many decent table wines are available at very reasonable prices. Although some people may prefer to use the higher-priced wines for cooking, the less expensive wines do produce fabulous results.

## White Wine

White wines tend to be the most versatile for flavoring and cooking. They are generally light in body with a delicate nature, are easily flavored, and, since they do not add color, can be used in just about any recipe.

The white wines used for flavored mixtures in this book are Chardonnay (dry and fruity), Chablis Blanc (very dry and woodsy), and Rhine (sweet and crisp). Although these wines have different characteristics, they can be used interchangeably. The Rhine imparts a sweeter taste than the Chablis Blanc, yet both are suitable for many of the recipes in this book, as is the Chardonnay.

The adage "white with fish, red with meat" does hold true to a certain degree when cooking with wine, simply because white wine will not color food. Chicken, fish, pasta, and light-colored vegetables are good candidates for white-wine mixtures. There are exceptions, though, and depending on the other ingredients, the cooking technique, and the final appearance of the food, a rosé or a red may be used. As an example, the Chicken Merlot with Caramelized Onions is a beautiful presentation of chicken and onions sautéed to a rosy brown.

## Red Wine

Red wines are hearty and flavorful, imparting a mellow richness, especially to meat, beans, tomatoes, and berries. The wines used to prepare the flavored mixtures are Burgundy (robust), Pinot Noir (tart and mildly fruity), Merlot (dense, smooth, and woodsy), and Cabernet Sauvignon (semidry and fruity).

Once again, depending on the ingredients and the cooking methods, the wines are interchangeable, and each will impart a slightly different flavor. The Peppered Pork Steaks with Pinot Noir Sauce would be just as flavorful made with the Rosemary and Garlic Burgundy or the Parsley and Savory Merlot wine mixture.

Since red wine does add color, it's best not to use these flavored wine mixtures when preparing light-colored foods. Three splendid exceptions, however, are the previously mentioned Chicken Merlot with Caramelized Onions, the Ricotta Salata Crostini, and the Bow-Tie Pasta Salad. So feel free to experiment, using these recipes as guidelines and keeping in mind that anything you cook in red wine will take on a deep mauve hue.

## Rosé

Rosé wines are sweet and slightly sparkling, a good alternative to the subtle white wines and the heavier red wines. They work well with all foods but will add a delicate lavender pink to light-colored foods. An example is the Herbal Wine Rice Pilaf made with the Chervil and Marjoram Rosé mixture. It is extremely tasty and pretty to look at, but pink rice is quite unusual. You may want to serve this dish to your more avant-garde friends.

As with the other mixtures, flavored rosé can also be used in different recipes. Try the Caramelized Carrots with the Mixed Herbs and Garlic Rosé, or the Parsley and Sage Chardonnay in the Vegetable Pot Pie. Once again, the slight variations in seasonings will result in some very tasty dishes.

In addition to the "basic rosé" used in the recipes provided, you can experiment with Grenache Rosé and White Zinfandel. 🍇

# Chapter Two
# Flavoring Wine

*Come, come; good wine is a good familiar
creature if it be well used.*

— William Shakespeare

Wines are an ideal base to flavor. With a lower acid content than vinegar, and less fat than oil, they offer the perfect alternative to both and impart a delicately seasoned, mellow flavor to the food. Since the wine absorbs the flavorings and permeates the food while cooking, the flavors are richer and more distinct. Most of the wine mixtures were developed using an assortment of herbs, but a few spice-wine, fruit-wine, and vegetable-wine mixtures are included.

## Process for Flavoring Wines

To make the flavored wines, you'll need the proper equipment — about a dozen one-pint or one-quart canning jars with lids, and measuring cups and spoons. That's it. Later on, you'll need a fine-mesh wire strainer to remove the flavorings from the mixture before using it in cooking. If you plan on giving the flavored wines as gifts, you may want to start collecting some decorative one-pint bottles, even though canning jars work just as well. Canning jars are the easiest to fill with the herbs and other flavorings and provide easy access when removing a tablespoon or two for tasting.

Making flavored wines is very easy. Make sure the jars and lids are clean and dry. Place the flavoring ingredients in the jar, pour the wine over, cover, and set in a cool, dark place for at least a week before tasting. Wine mixtures made with fresh fruits and vegetables should be refrigerated. Stir the mixture before testing — there's no need to shake. The flavorings can be removed at any time, but it's best to keep them in the wine for at least several weeks. The mixture may taste or smell strong, but the flavor will blend with the other ingredients when cooking.

Wine acts as a preservative, so the wine mixtures will keep for at least three months and, most likely, a lot longer. If the mixture does not smell fresh, has heavy sediment at the bottom, or if mold is found on the flavorings or floating on the wine, discard the mixture.

## Using Flavored Wine

Strain the wine mixture before use. If you have leftover wine after cooking, clean and dry the rim of the jar and lid, recap, and store as usual. Since the herbs and other flavorings have been depleted of all flavor in the flavoring process, discard them after you use the wine. However, most fruits that have absorbed the wine can be used for purees and garnishes (depending on taste and appearance).

Some of the recipes include fresh herbs as an optional garnish. When adding fresh herbs to other recipes, be sure to use herbs that complement the herbs in the wine mixture, and add the fresh herbs just before serving.

Don't despair if you have a small amount of wine left after using it in a recipe. As you become more comfortable with cooking with the wine mixtures, you'll be reaching for that extra half cup for a salad dressing or marinade. You can also add more wine to the original mixture to dilute the flavor. Just remember that even though the mixture may be a heavily scented concoction in the jar, it will turn your recipe into a delicately seasoned, delightfully scented, flavorful dish.

## Preparing the Herbs, Spices, and Fruits for Flavoring

Although virtually any herb or combination of herbs can be used for flavoring wines, they must be fresh. If you have an herb garden, you should have a good supply. If you don't have an herb garden, or if you want to supplement what you have, fresh herbs are available at supermarkets, specialty grocery stores, and farmer's markets. You can experiment with dried herbs, but you will not get the same results.

Whether you use herbs from your garden or herbs from the store, thoroughly wash and dry them just before mixing with the wine. When selecting packaged herbs, buy the freshest you can and check them for mold and discoloration of leaves. Choose herbs that have more leaves and fewer flowers in the package. If possible, use the herbs the same day you buy them, but depending on their quality, you can store them in the refrigerator for a day or two. The leaves of the herbs will darken as the wine absorbs their oil. Basil leaves, however, have a tendency to blotch.

The spice wines use whole spices and seeds in their natural form. You don't have to crush the seeds, since the wine will absorb the flavorings. Just about any spice or seed can be used. Peppercorns, mustard, dill, coriander, and cumin seeds, cinnamon, and cloves are used in the recipes provided. The spices and seeds will soften as they contribute their flavors to the wine.

The fruit wines are delicious as drinks as well as in cooking. The fruits are washed, dried, and cut into quarters or eighths. Leave the peel on lemons, oranges, limes, peaches, nectarines, plums, apples, and any fruit that has an edible skin. Mangoes and kiwi, as with other fruits that are peeled before eating, should have their skins removed before adding the wine.

Vegetables must also be washed and dried, then seeded and sliced into appropriate-size pieces. All types of peppers and onions are suitable for flavoring wines. Dried peppers and tomatoes also work well. Some dried peppers that have been used for flavoring wine can be used in cooking the dish as well. Taste a small piece of the pepper to test its flavor.

Almost half of the wine mixtures contain either fresh or roasted garlic. For many people, garlic is a staple. If you are not a garlic lover, you can adjust the recipes to reduce the amount of garlic or omit it completely. You may want to conduct an experiment by making two versions of the same recipe, one with and one without garlic, to determine the effect of the garlic in the wine mixture and in the completed dish.

## Choosing the Wines

All the recipes provided in this book are made with relatively inexpensive wines. As mentioned earlier, each wine has its own characteristics, and the same wine in different price ranges will render different results. When developing your own recipes, work back from the main ingredient to determine your wine and flavorings. For example, when developing the recipe for Burgundy Beef Stew, the meat and wine were decided, then the flavorings were added to complement the dish.

The best way to make the mixtures is to prepare one large batch at a time. Buy three 750-milliliter bottles of wine, one each of white, red, and rosé, and at least six bunches of assorted herbs. Have about two heads of garlic available, several different spices, a few pieces of fruit, and some vegetables. Mix and match, noting measurements and ingredients, comments on wine before flavoring, and date made. Label your jars. Check weekly, jotting down notes as the mixture progresses. It's a fun, creative way to spend the afternoon, and the results are well worth it. You can also buy one bottle of wine and try three different-flavored mixtures — herbal, spicy, and sweet. Or, if you're more conservative, you can buy a bottle of wine and make a batch of just one flavor. Once you try the flavored wine in cooking, you'll be eager to experiment with more. 🍇

# Chapter Three
## The Wine Recipes

*I feel a recipe is only a theme,*
*which an intelligent cook can play each*
*time with a variation.*

— Madame Jehane Benoit

The following recipes offer an introduction to the endless possibilities of matching a wine to a flavoring. Some, no doubt, will become favorites that you will cook with repeatedly. Others you will adjust to your own culinary style. To help you get started, the wine-mixture recipes in Part One have been cross-referenced with the recipes in Part Two. Feel free to use any other suitable wine mixtures. For example, the Roasted Vegetable Sandwich with Dipping Sauce can be made with any of the white, red, or rosé herbal-wine mixtures and even a few of the spice-wine mixtures.

There are many wines you can experiment with, and tasting the wines before and after flavoring is just as enjoyable as sampling the completed dishes.🍇

Before you begin preparing the wine mixtures, consult this checklist of guidelines:

✔ Bottles or jars and lids must be clean and dry.

✔ Herbs, fruits, and vegetables must be rinsed and dried. Do not use if blemished.

✔ It's not necessary when using herbs to remove the leaves from the stem.

✔ Wash chives before chopping.

✔ All measurements for flavorings can be adjusted. Use more or less, according to your taste.

✔ Since the red wines are hardy, they may require more quantities of herbs and other flavorings and a longer time for the flavors to blend.

✔ Place the flavorings in the container first, then pour the wine over the contents.

✔ Wipe rims of glass jars, and cover tightly.

✔ Keep a journal, noting the date the mixture was made, what type of wine and flavorings were used, and the measurements.

✔ Label the jars.

✔ Store in a cool and dark or dimly lit place for at least a week before testing.

✔ Test wines by dipping a teaspoon into the mixture and tasting. You can also test by inhaling the aroma of the mixture.

✔ For best results, do not use the wine mixtures for at least two weeks. (The white wine mixures can be tested after one week.) The longer they are stored, the more intense the flavor will be.

✔ Refrigerate any mixtures made with fresh fruits and vegetables (lemon and lime mixed with herbs can be stored in a cool place). Garlic does not have to be refrigerated.

✔ When ready to use, pour the wine mixture through a fine-mesh wire strainer into a measuring cup. Discard flavorings.

✔ If storing any remaining mixture, wipe rim of jar or bottle before capping.

✔ Generally, if a recipe calls for fewer than 5 sprigs of an herb (5 to 6 inches long) and 1½ cups of wine, a 1-pint jar can be used.  Bulky stems and larger quantities will require a 1-quart jar.

## Roasted Red Pepper and Garlic Chardonnay Wine

    1  roasted red pepper (page 50)
    8  cloves roasted garlic (page 57)
    2  cups Chardonnay

Cut roasted pepper into six strips. Remove skin from roasted garlic, keeping cloves whole. Place pepper and garlic in a 1-quart jar. Pour wine over and cover. Refrigerate for at least 1 week before testing flavor.

▶ *Used in: Roasted Red Pepper, Roasted Garlic, and Cheese Cornbread (page 88); Oven-Baked Breaded Chicken with Roasted Red Pepper Mayonnaise (page 115)*

## Basil Chardonnay

    5  sprigs basil
  1½  cups Chardonnay

Place basil in a 1-quart jar. Pour wine over and cover. Store in a cool, dim place for at least 1 week before testing flavor.

▶ *Used in: Sun-Dried Tomato and Spinach Tart (page 55); Brussels Sprouts, Bacon, and Cheese Puff (page 109); Baked Marinated Chicken Tenders (page 45)*

# Berry Chardonnay

*This recipe can be used to make Berry Cordial and Berry Wine Punch. For Berry Cordial, let the mixture sit in the refrigerator for at least a month. Taste every week for desired consistency; the mixture should be slightly thick and sweet. Strain before pouring into glasses. For Berry Wine Punch, add equal parts of wine and club soda to the wine mixture to taste. You can strain before serving or leave the fruit in the wine.*

- 2 cups fresh raspberries, strawberries, or blackberries
- 1/2 cup sugar
- 2 cups Chardonnay

Pick over berries, wash, and drain. Place the berries in a 1-quart jar and sprinkle with sugar. Pour wine over and cover. Refrigerate for at least 2 weeks before testing flavor.

# Orange Mango Chardonnay

- 1/2 orange, cut into 4 segments
- 1/2 mango, peeled and cut into 4 slices
- 3 1/2 cups Chardonnay

Place orange and mango in a 1-quart jar. Pour wine over and cover. Refrigerate for at least 2 weeks before testing flavor.

▶ *Used in: Marinade (page 75); Rice Custard with Fruit Topping (page 138)*

# Raspberry Chardonnay

- 1 package (10 ounces) frozen raspberries, defrosted, with juice
- 1 1/2 cups Chardonnay

Pour raspberries and juice into a 1-quart jar. Pour wine over and cover. Refrigerate for at least 2 weeks before testing flavor.

▶ *Used in: Red Berry Soup (page 63)*

## Mixed Herbs and Garlic Chardonnay

2–3  sprigs each chervil, parsley, sage, tarragon, and thyme
3  cloves garlic, peeled
1½  cups Chardonnay

Place chervil, parsley, sage, tarragon, thyme, and garlic in a 1-quart jar. Pour wine over and cover. Store in a cool, dim place for at least 1 week before testing flavor.

▶ *Used in: Savory Wine Pastry Puffs (page 51); Polenta with Roasted Red Pepper Goat Cheese (page 87)*

## Rosemary and Garlic Chardonnay

3  sprigs rosemary
2  cloves garlic, peeled and quartered
1½  cups Chardonnay

Place rosemary and garlic in a 1-pint jar. Pour wine over and cover. Store in a cool, dim place for at least 1 week before testing flavor.

▶ *Used in: White Bean Dip (page 58); Onion and Zucchini Tart (page 95); Sautéed Scallop Puffs (page 130)*

## Parsley and Sage Chardonnay

5  sprigs parsley
3  sprigs sage
1½  cups Chardonnay

Place parsley and sage in a 1-quart jar. Pour wine over and cover. Store in a cool, dim place for at least 1 week before testing flavor.

▶ *Used in: Spinach and Roasted Garlic Timbales (page 106); Creamy Cauliflower Casserole (page 108); Sautéed Chicken with Herbal Wine Sauce (page 117)*

# Italian Herb Chardonnay

    6   sprigs oregano
    3   sprigs basil
    3   cloves garlic, peeled
1½   cups Chardonnay

Place oregano, basil, and garlic in a 1-quart jar. Pour wine over and cover. Store in a cool, dim place for at least 1 week before testing flavor.

▶ *Used in: Marinade (page 75); Herbal Cheese Rice Balls (page 89); Herb and Garlic Mashed Potatoes (page 98); Chicken-Stuffed Red Pepper Halves (page 118)*


# Sage and Roasted Garlic Chardonnay

3–4   sprigs sage
    6   cloves roasted garlic
2½   cups Chardonnay

Place sage in a 1-quart jar. Remove skin from garlic, keeping the cloves whole, and add to jar. Pour wine over and cover. Store in a cool, dim place for at least 1 week before testing flavor.

▶ *Used in: Marinade (page 75); Caramelized Onions, Roasted Yellow Peppers, and Roasted Garlic Ricotta Pizza (page 50); Ham and Vegetable Salad (page 69)*


# Oregano, Fennel, and Garlic Chardonnay

    4   sprigs oregano
    2   teaspoons fennel seeds
    2   cloves garlic
1½   cups Chardonnay

Place oregano, fennel seeds, and garlic in a 1-pint jar. Pour wine over and cover. Store in a cool, dim place for at least 2 weeks before testing flavor.

▶ *Used in: Baked Stuffed Clams (page 60); Stuffed Vidalia Onions (page 105)*

## Thai Pepper Chardonnay

    2   Thai peppers (or other hot peppers)
  1½  cups Chardonnay

Cut stems off peppers and place in a 1-pint jar. Pour wine over and cover. Refrigerate at least 1 week before testing flavor.

▶ *Used in: Onion, Green Chili, and Cheese Muffins (page 52); Beef and Broccoli Stir-Fry (page 123)*


## Double Red Pepper Chablis Blanc

  ½  roasted red pepper (page 50)
  1  teaspoon red pepper flakes
 1½  cups Chablis Blanc

Slice roasted pepper into four pieces; place with pepper flakes in a 1-pint jar. Pour wine over and cover. Refrigerate for at least 2 weeks before testing flavor.

▶ *Used in: Ravioli with Broccoli (page 84)*


## Parsley and Garlic Chablis Blanc

  6  sprigs parsley
  4  cloves garlic
  2  cups Chablis Blanc

Place parsley and garlic in a 1-quart jar. Pour wine over and cover. Store in a cool, dim place for at least 1 week before testing flavor.

▶ *Used in: Florentine Stuffed Mushrooms (page 59); Broccoli Soup (page 63); Chicken Salad with Sun-Dried Tomatoes, Scallions, and Parsley (page 73); Scallop Cakes (page 131)*

# Basil and Garlic Chablis Blanc

> 5  sprigs basil
> 3  cloves garlic
> 2  cups Chablis Blanc

Place basil and garlic in a 1-quart jar. Pour wine over and cover. Store in a cool, dim place for at least 1 week before testing flavor.

▶ *Used in: Basil and Garlic Focaccia with Sautéed Sweet Peppers (page 48); Fettuccine with Shrimp and Artichoke Sauce (page 85); Breaded Scallops with Basil and Garlic Mayonnaise (page 134)*


# Rosemary Chablis Blanc

> 2–3  sprigs rosemary
> 2½  cups Chablis Blanc

Place rosemary in a 1-quart jar. Pour wine over and cover. Store in a cool, dark place for at least 1 week before testing flavor.

▶ *Used in: Baked Custard Crepe Cups (page 94); Herb-Baked Potatoes au Gratin (page 98)*


# Mixed Herb Chablis Blanc

> 5  sprigs tarragon
> 4  sprigs thyme
> 4  sprigs parsley
> 2  cups Chablis Blanc

Place tarragon, thyme, and parsley in a 1-quart glass container. Pour wine over and cover. Store in a cool, dim place for at least 2 weeks before testing flavor.

▶ *Used in: Herbed Rice and Cheese Soufflé (page 93); Chicken Pot Pie in Pastry Crust (page 114)*

# Basil, Fennel, and Garlic Chablis Blanc

> 4 sprigs basil
> 5 sprigs fennel
> 4 cloves garlic, peeled
> 2 cups Chablis Blanc

Place basil, fennel, and garlic in a 1-quart jar. Pour wine over and cover. Store in a cool, dim place for at least 2 weeks before testing flavor.

▶ *Used in: Light Béchamel Sauce (page 78); Lasagne Bundles (page 86); Marinated Smoked Mushrooms (page 107)*

# Herb, Lemon, and Garlic Chablis Blanc

> 4 sprigs chervil
> 3 sprigs sage
> ½ lemon
> 3 cloves garlic, peeled
> 2 cups Chablis Blanc

Place chervil and sage in a 1-quart jar. Cut lemon into two pieces and each garlic clove into two pieces, and add to jar. Pour wine over and cover. Store in a cool, dark place for at least 2 weeks before testing flavor.

▶ *Used in: Breaded Shrimp (page 129); Herbal Lemon Stuffed Fillets (page 133)*

# Peach Chablis Blanc

> 1 can (28 ounces) sliced peaches in light syrup
> ½ cup Chablis Blanc

Drain peaches, reserving ¼ cup of syrup for wine mixture. Place peaches and reserved syrup in a 2-quart jar. Pour wine over and cover. Refrigerate for at least 2 weeks before testing flavor.

▶ *Used in: Peach and Almond Cobbler (page 143)*

# Lemon Dill Rhine Wine

|   |   |
|---|---|
| 6 | sprigs dill |
| 1/4 | wedge lemon |
| 1 1/2 | cups Rhine wine |

Place dill and lemon in a 1-pint jar. Pour wine over and cover. Store in a cool, dim place for at least 1 week before testing flavor.

▶ *Used in: Broccoli and Monterey Jack Quiche (page 96); Seafood Crepes (page 135)*


# Parsley, Chive, and Garlic Rhine Wine

|   |   |
|---|---|
| 4 | sprigs parsley |
| 1/2 | cup snipped chives (1/2-inch pieces) |
| 2 | cloves garlic, peeled and quartered |
| 2 | cups Rhine wine |

Place parsley, chives, and garlic in a 1-quart jar. Pour wine over and cover. Store in a cool, dim place for at least 1 week before testing flavor.

▶ *Used in: Broccoli Stromboli (page 46); Bean and Spinach Soup (page 66); Marinated London Broil (page 119)*


# Cilantro, Lime, and Garlic Rhine Wine

|   |   |
|---|---|
| 4 | sprigs cilantro |
| 1/4 | wedge lime |
| 3 | cloves garlic, sliced |
| 1 1/2 | cups Rhine wine |

Place cilantro, lime, and garlic in a 1-pint jar. Pour wine over and cover. Store in a cool, dim place for at least 1 week before testing flavor.

▶ *Used in: Chicken Fajitas with Roasted Red and Yellow Peppers (page 111); Shrimp Nachos (page 128)*

# Parsley, Chive, and Lemon Rhine Wine

    5   sprigs parsley
  1/2  cup snipped chives (2-inch pieces)
  1/2  lemon
    2   cups Rhine wine

Cut lemon in half. Place parsley, chives, and lemon in a 1-quart jar. Pour wine over and cover. Store in a cool, dry place for at least 1 week before testing flavor.

▶ *Used in: Steamed Broccoli (page 103); Breaded Broccoli (page 103); Oven-Baked Fish Fillets (page 134)*

# Chervil, Chive, and Dill Rhine Wine

    5   sprigs chervil
  1/2  cup snipped chives (2-inch pieces)
    2   teaspoons dill seed
    2   cups Rhine wine

Place chervil, chives, and dill seed in a 1-quart jar. Pour wine over and cover. Store in a cool, dim place for at least 1 week before testing flavor.

▶ *Used in: Potato and Cauliflower Soup with Scallions (page 64); Broiled Shrimp (page 129)*

# Coriander and Peppercorn Rhine Wine

    1   teaspoon coriander seeds
    1   teaspoon peppercorns
    1   cup Rhine wine

Place coriander seeds and peppercorns in a 1-pint jar. Pour wine over and cover. Store in a cool, dim place for at least 2 weeks before testing flavor.

▶ *Used in: Onion and Brown Sugar Relish (page 81); Fish Fillets with Caramelized Onion Wine Sauce (page 132)*

## Sesame, Chili Pepper, and Garlic Rhine Wine

2 teaspoons sesame seeds
5 dried red chili peppers
2 cloves garlic, peeled
1½ cups Rhine wine

Place sesame seeds, chili peppers, and garlic in a 1-pint jar. Pour wine over and cover. Store in a cool, dim place for at least 2 weeks before testing flavor.

▶ *Used in: Spicy Sesame Chicken (page 44)*

## Orange Rhine Wine

1 large navel orange
2 cups Rhine wine

Cut orange into six wedges and place in a 1-quart jar. Pour wine over and cover. Refrigerate for at least 2 weeks before testing flavor.

▶ *Used in: Orange Tea Loaf (page 144)*

## Oregano and Garlic Burgundy

6   sprigs oregano
4   cloves garlic, peeled and halved
1½  cups Burgundy

Place oregano and garlic in a 1-quart jar. Pour wine over and cover. Store in a cool, dim place for at least 2 weeks before testing flavor.

▶ *Used in: Sun-Dried Tomato Pastry Swirls (page 53); Burgundy Tomato and Roasted Garlic Sauce (page 80)*

## Mixed Herbs and Garlic Burgundy

4   sprigs parsley
4   sprigs basil
4   sprigs dill
1   cup snipped chives (2-inch pieces)
3   cloves garlic, peeled
2   cups Burgundy

Place parsley, basil, dill, chives, and garlic in a 1-quart jar. Pour wine over and cover. Store in a cool, dark place for at least 2 weeks before testing flavor.

▶ *Used in: Sun-Dried Tomato and Roasted Garlic Cheese Spread (page 56); Sun-Dried Tomato and Roasted Garlic Dip (page 57)*

## Garlic and Chive Burgundy

4   cloves garlic, peeled
1   cup snipped chives (1-inch pieces)
1½  cups Burgundy

Place garlic and chives in a 1-pint jar. Pour wine over and cover. Store in a cool, dark place for at least 2 weeks before testing flavor.

▶ *Used in: Marinade (page 76); Roma Tomato and Onion Relish (page 82)*

# Rosemary and Garlic Burgundy

    4–5   sprigs rosemary
      4   cloves garlic, peeled and halved
    1½   cups Burgundy

Place rosemary and garlic in a 1-pint jar. Pour wine over and cover. Store in a cool, dark place for at least 2 weeks before testing flavor.

▶ *Used in: Marinade (page 77); Basic Tomato Sauce (page 79)*

# Thyme and Marjoram Burgundy

    4–5   sprigs thyme
    4–5   sprigs marjoram
      2   cups Burgundy

Place thyme and marjoram in a 1-quart jar. Pour wine over and cover. Store in a cool, dark place for at least 2 weeks before testing flavor.

▶ *Used in: Burgundy Beef Stew (page 121); Ham Steaks with Burgundy Honey Mustard Sauce (page 126)*

# Basil, Parsley, and Garlic Burgundy

    6   sprigs basil
    5   sprigs parsley
    4   cloves garlic, peeled
    2   cups Burgundy

Place basil, parsley, and garlic in a 1-quart jar. Pour wine over and cover. Store in a cool, dark place for at least 2 weeks before testing flavor.

▶ *Used in: Ricotta Salata Crostini (page 61); Vegetable Soup with Roasted Garlic Bread (page 65); Panzanella (page 69)*

# Mixed Herb Burgundy

4–5 sprigs marjoram
4–5 sprigs thyme
3–4 sprigs parsley
3–4 sprigs tarragon
2–3 sprigs sage
2 cups Burgundy

Place marjoram, thyme, parsley, tarragon, and sage in a 1-quart jar. Pour wine over and cover. Store in a cool, dark place for at least 2 weeks before testing flavor.

▶ *Used in: Sun-Dried Tomato and Cheese Torta (page 54); Three-Bean Chili (page 91)*

# Parsley and Savory Merlot

6 sprigs parsley
8 sprigs savory
1½ cups Merlot

Place parsley and savory in a 1-quart jar. Pour wine over and cover. Store in a cool, dark place for at least 2 weeks before testing flavor.

▶ *Used in: Bow-Tie Pasta Salad (page 71); Marinade (page 77); Stuffed Marinated Flank Steak (page 120)*

# Mixed Herbs and Garlic Merlot

8 sprigs fennel
5 sprigs basil
3 sprigs savory
4 cloves garlic, peeled
2 cups Merlot

Place fennel, basil, savory, and garlic in a 1-quart jar. Pour wine over and cover. Store in a cool, dark place for at least 2 weeks before testing flavor.

▶ *Used in: Ratatouille (page 99); Chicken Merlot with Caramelized Onions (page 113)*

# Sun-Dried Tomato and Garlic Merlot

½ cup (10–12 pieces) sun-dried tomatoes (not packed in oil)
3 cloves garlic, peeled
1 cup Merlot

Place tomatoes and garlic in a 1-pint jar. Pour wine over and cover. Store for at least 2 weeks before testing flavor.

▶ *Used in: Baked Chicken Sandwich (page 116); Beef and Sun-Dried Tomatoes (page 122)*

# Raspberry Merlot

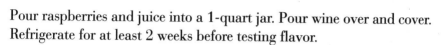

1½ cups frozen raspberries, defrosted, with juice
1 cup Merlot

Pour raspberries and juice into a 1-quart jar. Pour wine over and cover. Refrigerate for at least 2 weeks before testing flavor.

▶ *Used in: Nectarine and Mixed Berry Sorbet (page 140); Raspberry Merlot Chocolate Mousse Cake (page 142)*

# Chili Pepper and Garlic Pinot Noir

12–14 dried red chili peppers
4 cloves garlic, peeled
2 teaspoons cumin seeds
2½ cups Pinot Noir

Place chili peppers, garlic, and cumin seeds in a 1-quart jar. Pour wine over and cover. Store in a cool, dim place for at least 2 weeks before testing flavor.

▶ *Used in: Spicy Pinto Beans (page 92)*

# Mustard and Garlic Pinot Noir

2 teaspoons mustard seeds
2 cloves garlic, peeled
1 cup Pinot Noir

Place mustard seeds and garlic in a 1-pint jar. Pour wine over and cover. Store in a cool, dim place for at least 2 weeks before testing flavor.

▶ *Used in: Peppered Pork Steaks with Pinot Noir Sauce (page 125)*

# Spiced Cinnamon Pinot Noir

2 sticks cinnamon
4 cloves
1 cup Pinot Noir

Place cinnamon and cloves in a 1-pint jar. Pour wine over and cover. Store in a cool, dim place for at least 2 weeks before testing flavor.

▶ *Used in: Spiced Nectarine Tart (page 139); Fruit in Spiced Wine Syrup (page 140); Hazelnut Gâteau (page 141)*

# Thyme, Tarragon, and Chive Cabernet Sauvignon

4 sprigs thyme
4 sprigs tarragon
½ cup snipped chives (2-inch pieces)
2 cups Cabernet Sauvignon

Place thyme, tarragon, and chives in a 1-quart jar. Pour wine over and cover. Store in a cool, dim place for at least 2 weeks before testing flavor.

▶ *Used in: Greek Potato Salad (page 68); Vegetable-Stuffed Eggplant (page 101)*

# Chili Pepper Cabernet Sauvignon

        12    red chili peppers
         1    cup Cabernet Sauvignon

Place chili peppers in a 1-pint jar. Pour wine over and cover. Store in a cool, dim place for at least 2 weeks before testing flavor.

▶ *Used in: Black Bean, Tomato, and Onion Salad (page 72)*


# Raspberry Cabernet Sauvignon

        1¼    cups frozen raspberries
        1½    cups Cabernet Sauvignon

Place frozen raspberries in a 1-quart jar. Pour wine over and cover. Refrigerate for at least 2 weeks before testing flavor.

▶ *Used in: Chocolate Raspberry Pudding or Mousse (page 145)*


# Sweet Cherry Cabernet Sauvignon

         1    can (16 ounces) sweet cherries in heavy syrup
        ½     cup Cabernet Sauvignon

Pour cherries and syrup into a 1-quart jar. Pour wine over and cover. Refrigerate for at least 2 weeks before testing flavor.

▶ *Used in: Black Forest Cherry Cake (page 146)*

# Rosé Recipes

## Sage and Garlic Rosé

       4  sprigs sage
       3  cloves garlic, peeled
    1½  cups rosé

Place sage and garlic in a 1-pint jar. Pour wine over and cover. Store in a cool, dim place for at least 2 weeks before testing flavor.

▶ *Used in: Green Beans and Mushroom Salad (page 71); Roasted Vegetable Sandwich with Dipping Sauce (page 102)*


## Parsley and Garlic Rosé

       6  sprigs parsley
       3  cloves garlic, peeled
       2  cups rosé

Place parsley and garlic in a 1-quart jar. Pour wine over and cover. Store in a cool, dim place for at least 2 weeks before testing flavor.

▶ *Used in: Marinade (page 76); Chicken Rosé with Parsley and Garlic Focaccia (page 112)*


## Chervil and Marjoram Rosé

       5  sprigs chervil
       4  sprigs marjoram
    1½  cups rosé

Place chervil and marjoram in a 1-quart jar. Pour wine over and cover. Store in a cool, dim place for at least 2 weeks before testing flavor.

▶ *Used in: Tomato and Shrimp Gazpacho with Roasted Garlic Sour Cream (page 62); Herbal Wine Rice Pilaf (page 90)*

# Mixed Herbs and Garlic Rosé

    4   sprigs parsley
    4   sprigs fennel
    3   sprigs basil
    3   sprigs savory
    3   cloves garlic, peeled
    2   cups rosé

Place parsley, fennel, basil, savory, and garlic in a 1-quart jar. Pour wine over and cover. Store in a cool, dim place for at least 2 weeks before testing flavor.

▶ *Used in: Vegetable Pot Pie (page 100); Green Beans and Bread Crumbs (page 107)*

# Basil and Garlic Rosé

    5   sprigs basil
    3   cloves garlic, peeled
    2   cups rosé

Place basil and garlic in a 1-quart jar. Pour wine over and cover. Store in a cool, dim place for at least 2 weeks before testing flavor.

▶ *Used in: Broccoli Salad (page 70); Pork Strips and Onion Pain Bagnet (page 124)*

# Parsley and Savory Rosé

    5   sprigs parsley
    6   sprigs savory
  1½  cups rosé

Place parsley and savory in a 1-quart jar. Pour wine over and cover. Store in a cool, dim place for at least 2 weeks before testing flavor.

▶ *Used in: Checkerboard Pasta Salad (page 70); Caramelized Carrots (page 104)*

## Basil, Fennel, and Garlic Rosé

       4  sprigs basil
       4  sprigs fennel
       3  cloves garlic, peeled
    1½  cups rosé

Place basil, fennel, and garlic in a 1-quart jar. Pour wine over and cover.
Store in a cool, dim place for at least 2 weeks before testing flavor.

▶ *Used in: Spinach Salad (page 72); Fresh Tomato Sauce (page 79)*

## Rosemary and Black Peppercorn Rosé

    3–4  sprigs rosemary
       1  tablespoon black peppercorns
       2  cups rosé

Place rosemary and peppercorns in a 1-quart jar. Pour wine over and cover.
Store in a cool, dim place for at least 2 weeks before testing flavor.

▶ *Used in: Marinade (page 76); Caramelized Onions (page 104)*

## Double Red Pepper Rosé

1   roasted red pepper (page 50)
1   tablespoon red pepper flakes
2   cups rosé

Slice roasted pepper into six pieces and place in a 1-quart jar. Sprinkle with red pepper flakes. Pour wine over and cover. Refrigerate for at least 2 weeks before testing flavor.

▶ *Used in: Red Pesto Sauce (page 80)*

## Strawberry Rosé

1   cup halved strawberries
2   cups rosé

Place strawberries in a 1-quart jar. Pour wine over and cover. Refrigerate for at least 2 weeks before testing flavor.

▶ *Used in: Strawberry Rosé Parfait (page 137)*

# Chapter Four

## Gift Ideas

*Fan the sinking flame of familiarity with the
wing of friendship; and pass the rosy wine.*

— Charles Dickens

The flavored wine mixtures make wonderful gifts for anyone who cooks. A wine mixture with a recipe written on a decorative card and all or some of the ingredients can be packaged together in a number of combinations to create a memorable gift.

Match the gift to fit the recipient. A family that loves chili would appreciate the ingredients and the recipe for Three-Bean Chili presented in a ceramic chili pot. Give a vegetarian a basketful of vegetables, the recipe, and the accompaniments for Roasted Vegetable Sandwich with Dipping Sauce. Or give a seafood lover a package or two of natural baking shells, the wine mixture, a few cans of chopped clams, and the recipe for Baked Stuffed Clams in a fishnet bag.

Gifts can range from very simple and inexpensive to quite elaborate. The easiest is a bottle or jar of an herbal wine, with the recipe attached by ribbon or raffia on a hangtag. A few different jars of the flavored mixtures with recipes for each, or with a copy of this book, in a decorative bag or basket is a thoughtful gift for beginning and accomplished cooks. 🍇

When preparing your gifts keep the following in mind:

✔ You can use the canning jars or any decorative bottle or jar.

✔ Leave the herbs in the mixture for a decorative look.

✔ Make the container part of the gift. Use decorative bags in assorted sizes, baskets, bowls, or a variety of cookware. Secure the bottoms of large bags with a piece of heavy cardboard cut to fit the bottom and folded to come halfway up the narrow sides.

✔ Use a shredded filler to cushion the ingredients and to fill in empty spaces.

✔ Always include a recipe or two, written on a decorative note or recipe card. Better yet, include this book in the gift package.

✔ Jars and bottles can be decorated with dried or silk flowers or small wreaths. The caps can be covered with fabric and tied with ribbons or raffia.

✔ Adding a fine-mesh wire strainer is a nice touch.

The following gift ideas will help get you started:

### Mushroom Gift Package
*Basil, Fennel, and Garlic Chablis Blanc*
*A package of dried mushrooms*
*Liquid Smoke*
*The recipe for Marinated Smoked Mushrooms*

### Polenta Gift Package
*Mixed Herbs and Garlic Chardonnay*
*A package of cornmeal*
*Grated Parmesan*
*A jar of roasted peppers or one fresh red pepper*
*The recipe for Polenta with Roasted Red Pepper Goat Cheese*

## Rice Custard Gift Package

*Orange Mango Chardonnay*
*A package of rice*
*An orange, mango, and kiwi*
*A set of parfait glasses*
*The recipe for Rice Custard with Fruit Topping*

## Onion Gift Package

*Oregano, Fennel, and Garlic Chardonnay*
*Vidalia onions*
*The recipe for Stuffed Vidalia Onions*

## Clam Gift Package

*Oregano, Fennel, and Garlic Chardonnay*
*Two cans of chopped clams*
*A package or two of natural baking shells*
*The recipe for Baked Stuffed Clams*

## Pasta Gift Package

*Parsley and Savory Merlot*
*A box of bow-tie pasta*
*Green pepper and plum tomatoes*
*Fresh parsley*
*Pasta bowl*
*The recipe for Bow-Tie Pasta Salad*

## Panzanella Gift Package

*Basil, Parsley, and Garlic Burgundy*
*Plum tomatoes and red onion*
*Small bottle of olive oil*
*Loaf of crusty sesame bread*
*Salad bowl*
*The recipe for Panzanella*

## Chili Gift Package

*Mixed Herb Burgundy*
*Dried black, kidney, and white beans*
*Can of diced green chilies*
*Can of crushed tomatoes*
*Dried chili peppers*
*Ceramic chili pot*
*Recipe for Three-Bean Chili*

## Nectarine Tart Gift Package

*Spiced Cinnamon Pinot Noir*
*A pound of nectarines*
*Tart pan*
*Recipe for Spiced Nectarine Tart*

## Roasted Vegetable Sandwich Gift Package

*Sage and Garlic Rosé*
*Zucchini and eggplant*
*Tomatoes and red onion*
*Head of garlic*
*Small bottle of olive oil*
*Parmesan*
*Loaf of crusty sesame bread*
*Recipe for Roasted Vegetable Sandwich with Dipping Sauce*

## Focaccia Gift Package

*Parsley and Garlic Rosé*
*Yeast*
*Ceramic bowl and wooden spoon*
*Recipe for Chicken Rosé with Parsley and Garlic Focaccia*

## Caramelized Carrot Gift Package

*Parsley and Savory Rosé*
*Farm-fresh carrots with lots of greenery*
*Decorative mesh or canvas bag*
*Recipe for Caramelized Carrots*

# Part Two

# Cooking with Flavored Wines

Cooking with wine is not a novel concept, but cooking with flavored wine offers a new dimension in preparing food. The recipes in this section have been developed to be prepared with, and are cross-referenced to, the flavored wine mixtures from Part One. Keep in mind, though, that many mixtures can be substituted. So even though the recipe for Oven-Baked Fish Fillets calls for the Coriander and Peppercorn Rhine Wine, you can use the Basil and Garlic Chablis Blanc or the Roasted Red Pepper and Garlic Chardonnay or any other mixture that suits your taste, including one that you have created. Each wine mixture will add a distinct flavor to the dish and will provide you with a continuous source of new recipes to try.

You may notice that salt is not listed as an ingredient in any of the recipes. The wine and seasonings in the wine add the flavor, along with natural sodium in the food. If you are accustomed to using salt, wait until the food is cooked and you have tasted it. Sprinkle on salt if you think it's required.

The taste testers for these recipes were an extremely diverse group, ranging from fast-food junkies to meat-and-potato people and gourmets. Salt was not offered at the table, and everyone was surprised when told that salt had not been added to the recipes. Many commented on how tasty the food was and how they could detect the many different flavors attributed to each dish. 🍇

# Chapter Five

# About the Ingredients

*That he may bring food out of the earth and wine that*
*maketh glad the heart of man and oil to make him a cheerful*
*countenance and bread to strengthen man's heart.*

— Prayer Book, 1662

The finest ingredients produce the most successful recipes. This chapter provides information on some of the ingredients most frequently used.

Many of the recipes call for a small amount of butter or margarine. All of the recipes in this collection were made with margarine (70 percent vegetable-oil spread). Low-fat margarine can be substituted when sautéing and preparing sauces. Do not use spreads in a tub or substitute low-fat margarine in baking.

Olive oil and canola oil are also listed as ingredients. You can substitute corn oil or peanut oil for the canola oil, depending on the dish, but do not substitute any other oil for the olive oil. Use a good-quality olive oil, because it really does make a difference. You can use an extra-virgin or extra-light olive oil in the salad dressings, but it isn't necessary.

Recipes calling for cream cheese, sour cream, and mayonnaise can also use the light versions. Neufchâtel cheese or a fat-free version can replace cream cheese. A good-quality name-brand fat-free sour cream is an excellent substitute for regular sour cream, and a low-fat mayonnaise works just as well as regular mayonnaise.

Freshly ground black pepper is called for in just about every recipe. You can also use green or white pepper. If you are not in the habit of grinding pepper, now would be a good time to try. It's another ingredient that contributes a lot to the recipe, especially if you like the spicy tang of pepper in food.

In recipes that call for flavored bread crumbs, you can use store-bought crumbs or make your own (see page 38). Or try flavored breads from the bakery or grocery store. Sun-dried tomato bread and pesto bread are just two examples of the types you can use to make the flavored crumbs.

In recipes that require crusty sesame bread or crusty bread, buy an unsliced loaf of any good-quality bread at a bakery or in the bakery section of the supermarket or specialty grocery store.

When using grated Parmesan use a good-quality, 100 percent cheese. Low-fat shredded cheese can be substituted for any of the other cheeses called for in the recipes.

For recipes that include sun-dried tomatoes, use packaged dried tomatoes. They are available in 3-ounce packages in the produce section of most supermarkets and specialty grocery stores. Do not use dried tomatoes packed in oil, since these tomatoes cannot be reconstituted and the seasonings in the oil will alter the taste of the dish.

Some recipes require peeled tomatoes. Peeling them is a breeze with this easy method. Place a tomato in a 2-quart saucepan and cover with water. Remove tomato. Bring water to a boil. Pour 1 cup of cold water and 1 cup of ice into a 1-quart bowl. One at a time, pierce the top of each tomato with a large fork and place in the boiling water. Let it sit for about a minute, then plunge the tomato into the ice water for another minute or so. Peel skin and discard.

The recipes for roasted peppers and roasted garlic, which are called for in many preparations in this book, are included in the appetizer section of Part Two.

One final note, not on the ingredients but in reference to a cooking method: Since wine mixtures are the basis of these recipes, sauces are a prominent feature in many of the dishes. The most flavorful sauces are made with the drippings from sautéed or roasted foods. In numerous recipes, you will see the term "deglaze." That is the technique for turning pan drippings into a heavenly melange of flavors in a sauce that accentuates each dish (see box above).🍇

## Flavored Bread Crumbs

Any leftover bread can be made into bread crumbs.

Place bread slices on a baking sheet and cook in a 200°F oven, turning several times, until both sides of the bread are firm and dry. Crush with a rolling pin, or grind into crumbs in a food processor. Label and store in a plastic container, tightly covered, in the refrigerator.

## Deglazing

To deglaze a pan simply means to add liquid to the pan and heat, stirring the liquid to loosen the bits and pieces attached to the pan. As you are stirring, the liquid will darken and thicken, incorporating the flavorful drippings and yielding a delectable sauce to pour over the cooked food or to serve as a dipping sauce.

Many of the recipes that use roasting as a cooking method call for deglazing the pan. Place the roasting pan on the stove, pour the wine into the roasting pan, and cook over medium heat, stirring until the sauce has thickened.

# Chapter Six
# Menus for Entertaining

*Strange to see how a good dinner and
feasting reconciles everybody.*

— Samuel Pepys

In preparing this book, numerous taste testers were recruited. While some sampled a single dish or several unrelated dishes, others shared an entire meal, from appetizer to dessert.

Since many of the recipes complemented each other so well, this chapter is devoted to menu suggestions. They offer a quick reference guide when you want to prepare an entire meal but don't have the time to plan it. Most dishes can be prepared earlier in the day, or even a day or two ahead, which is another time saver. Those dishes that cannot be prepared ahead are marked with an asterisk.

One last comment on the recipes in this book: When preparing the dishes, you will notice that the cooking aromas are incredibly delightful; however, that's just an introduction to the exceptional meal you will be savoring. Enjoy. 🍇

# Brunch Menus

### Summer Brunch

*Red Berry Soup (page 63)*
*Broccoli and Monterey Jack Quiche (page 96)*
*Onion and Zucchini Tart (page 95)*
*\*Panzanella (page 69)*
*Rice Custard with Fruit Topping (page 138)*

### Winter Brunch

*Baked Custard Crepe Cups (page 94)*
*Broccoli Stromboli (page 46)*
*\*Ham and Vegetable Salad (page 69)*
*Fruit in Spiced Wine Syrup (page 140)*

# Buffet Menus

### Spring Buffet

*Savory Wine Pastry Puffs (page 51)*
*Sun-Dried Tomato and Spinach Tart (page 55)*
*Baked Marinated Chicken Tenders (page 45)*
*Basil and Garlic Focaccia with Sautéed Sweet Peppers (page 48)*
*Spiced Nectarine Tart (page 139)*

### Autumn Buffet

*Florentine Stuffed Mushrooms (page 59)*
*Marinated London Broil (page 119)*
*Herb-Baked Potatoes au Gratin (page 98)*
*Green Beans and Bread Crumbs (page 107)*
*Raspberry Merlot Chocolate Mousse Cake (page 142)*

*Indicates dishes that cannot be prepared ahead.

# Lunch Menus

### Summer Lunch
*Sun-Dried Tomato Pastry Swirls (page 53)*
*Chicken Rosé with Parsley and Garlic Focaccia (page 112)*
*Broccoli Salad (page 70)*
*Strawberry Rosé Parfait (page 137)*

### Autumn Lunch
*Tomato and Shrimp Gazpacho with Roasted Garlic Sour Cream (page 62)*
*Pork Strips and Onion Pain Bagnet (page 124)*
*Checkerboard Pasta (page 70)*
*Spiced Nectarine Tart (page 139)*

### Winter Lunch
*Polenta with Roasted Red Pepper Goat Cheese (page 87)*
*Ravioli with Broccoli (page 84)*
*Black Bean, Tomato, and Onion Salad (page72)*
*Hazelnut Gâteau (page 141)*

### Spring Lunch
*Red Berry Soup (page 63)*
*\*Fettuccine with Shrimp and Artichoke Sauce (page 85)*
*Green Beans and Mushroom Salad (page 71)*
*Fruit in Spiced Wine Syrup (page 140)*

\*Indicates dishes that cannot be prepared ahead.

# Dinner Menus

## Summer Dinner

*Ricotta Salata Crostini (page 61)*
*Herbal Lemon Stuffed Fish Fillets (page 133)*
*Marinated Smoked Mushrooms (page 107)*
*Steamed Broccoli (page 103)*
*Nectarine and Mixed Berry Sorbet (page 140)*

## Autumn Dinner

*Sun-Dried Tomato and Cheese Torta (page 54)*
*Stuffed Marinated Flank Steak (page 120)*
*Spinach and Roasted Garlic Timbales (page 106)*
*Caramelized Carrots (page 104)*
*Raspberry Merlot Chocolate Mousse Cake (page 142)*

## Winter Dinner

*Potato and Cauliflower Soup with Scallions (page 64)*
*Burgundy Beef Stew (page 121)*
*Herbal Wine Rice Pilaf (page 90)*
*Fruit in Spiced Wine Syrup (page 140)*

## Spring Dinner

*Vegetable Soup with Roasted Garlic Bread (page 65)*
*Lasagne Bundles (page 86)*
*Breaded Broccoli (page 103)*
*Strawberry Rosé Parfait (page 137)*

*Indicates dishes that cannot be prepared ahead.

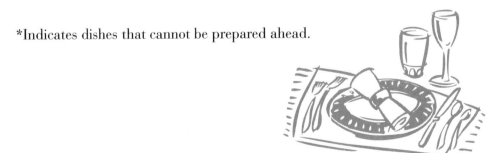

# Chapter Seven

# Appetizers and Soups

*A good meal ought to begin with hunger.*

— French Proverb

Whether a savory morsel or a soothing soup, the first course is meant to awaken the appetite. Always match the first course to the entrée, side dishes, and dessert to provide a blend of eye-appealing tasty dishes, and vary the texture of the foods to complement each other. See Chapter Six, "Menus for Entertaining," on page 39 for some suggestions.

Although the following recipes were specifically developed as first-course fare, the appetizers are wonderful for parties and snacks and the soups can become an entrée. Serve with a salad of vegetable, pasta, or fruit, and with muffins, croissants, or crusty bread for a satisfying meal. 🍇

# Spicy Sesame Chicken

*This is a good make-ahead dish, since the chicken can marinate up to one day before preparing. It can be made even spicier by adding more chili peppers from the wine mixture to the marinade. Chicken tenders cook quickly under the broiler, so keep a watchful eye on them. For a main dish, use chicken breasts and serve over rice.*

▶ *Yield: 6 servings as an appetizer, 4 as an entrée*

  1 cup Sesame, Chili Pepper, and Garlic Rhine Wine (page 21)
  1½ teaspoons sesame seed oil
  2 cloves garlic, crushed
  1 pound chicken tenders
  chili peppers from Sesame, Chili Pepper, and Garlic Rhine Wine (optional)
  sesame seeds

With a fork, mix ½ cup of the wine and sesame seed oil until well blended. Stir in crushed garlic. Place chicken in a 1-quart glass baking dish. Pour marinade over, and turn chicken pieces to coat on both sides. Add chili peppers, if desired. Cover with plastic wrap and refrigerate, marinating for at least 2 hours on each side.

Preheat broiler. Place chicken pieces in a rimmed baking sheet or baking pan. Sprinkle with sesame seeds. Cook under broiler until browned. Turn chicken pieces over, sprinkle with additional sesame seeds, and cook until browned.

Remove chicken to serving platter. Use remaining ½ cup wine to deglaze roasting pan, reducing liquid to a rich, brown, slightly thick sauce. Pour sauce into bowl and serve with chicken.

# Baked Marinated Chicken Tenders

*This recipe can be easily prepared and cooked a day ahead. Just reheat in the microwave at medium power for several minutes. Or serve cold.*

▶ *Yield: 4–6 servings*

- 1 pound chicken tenders
- ½ cup Basil Chardonnay (page 12)
- 2 tablespoons olive oil
- 2 cloves garlic, crushed
- 1 cup flavored bread crumbs (page 38)
  olive oil

Place chicken tenders in a small glass baking dish. Mix wine, oil, and garlic well, and pour over chicken. Turn to coat. Cover with plastic wrap and refrigerate, marinating at least 2 hours on each side.

Preheat oven to 375°F. Coat chicken tenders with bread crumbs. Pour olive oil into a rimmed baking pan to coat heavily. Place in oven to heat oil. When oil begins to sizzle, remove pan from oven. Place chicken in baking pan, return to oven, and bake, turning once, until browned on both sides, about 15 minutes. (You may need to add more oil during cooking.) Transfer chicken to serving platter.

# Broccoli Stromboli

*Wine in the dough adds a delicate flavor but requires a longer proofing time. Using a mixer with a dough hook saves time when kneading the flour mixture. After rising, the dough is wrapped around a filling of herb-flavored broccoli and cheese, then baked until the cheese melts and the crust is golden brown. Stromboli freezes well: Wrap tightly with a double layer of aluminum foil and use within 1 month. Defrost for about ½ hour before reheating at 300°F for about 45 minutes. You may want to cut the stromboli into 1-inch slices halfway through heating time to allow the center to cook through.*

▶ *Yield: 28–30 slices*

### Dough

1   cup Parsley, Chive, and Garlic Rhine Wine (page 19)
1   cup hot water
1   package active dry yeast
3   tablespoons olive oil
5   cups unbleached all-purpose flour

### Broccoli filling

1   pound fresh broccoli florets, rinsed well and chopped into 1-inch pieces
1   cup Parsley, Chive, and Garlic Rhine Wine
2   cups shredded cheese (any combination of Swiss, cheddar, Monterey Jack, or mozzarella)
    olive oil

**To make dough:** Combine wine and water in a large mixing bowl. Add yeast and let proof 10 to 15 minutes, or until yeast has dissolved. Add 2 tablespoons of the olive oil and 3 cups of the flour, and mix with a wooden spoon or dough hook until a sticky dough forms. Gradually add remaining 2 cups of flour, then knead with a dough hook about 5 minutes or by hand for 15 minutes, until dough is soft, smooth, and elastic. With remaining tablespoon of olive oil, coat a 2-quart glass or ceramic bowl and, with oiled fingertips, place the dough in the bowl, turning dough until completely coated. Cover with wax paper and set in a warm place to rise until doubled in bulk, about 1½ hours.

**To make broccoli filling:** While dough is rising, place broccoli in a 2-quart microwaveable dish and pour wine over. Cover with wax paper and cook at medium power in microwave for 5 minutes, stirring once midway through cooking time. Drain and cool.

On a lightly floured surface, spread dough to a 16 by 16-inch square. Cut dough in half and spread half of broccoli in the center of each piece. Sprinkle cheese evenly over broccoli. Gently roll each piece of dough lengthwise, sealing tightly and tucking ends under, keeping seam on bottom. Place seam side down on an oiled baking sheet. Brush with oil, cover with wax paper, and let rise ½ hour.

Preheat oven to 400°F. Brush stromboli with olive oil and bake for 30 minutes, or until crust is golden brown. Let cool slightly before cutting with a serrated knife into 1-inch slices.

Active dry yeast requires a temperature between 105°F and 115°F to dissolve. The wine-and-hot–water mixture provides the lukewarm temperature that yeast needs to start the leavening process. When combined with flour, the yeast produces carbon dioxide, causing the dough to rise.

# Basil and Garlic Focaccia with Sautéed Sweet Peppers

*Basil and Garlic Chablis Blanc gently seasons the focaccia, which complements the sautéed peppers. The focaccia recipe makes two 9-inch or 10-inch loaves. The extra focaccia can be wrapped tightly in foil and frozen. Defrost before reheating at 300°F for 15 minutes. The recipe for the sautéed sweet peppers will fill or top one focaccia.*

▶ *Yield: 6–12 servings*

### Focaccia

| | |
|---|---|
| 1½ | cups Basil and Garlic Chablis Blanc (page 17) |
| 1 | package active dry yeast |
| 1 | teaspoon sugar |
| ½ | cup olive oil |
| 5½ | cups unbleached all-purpose flour |

### Sautéed Peppers

| | |
|---|---|
| 3 | sweet red peppers |
| 2 | sweet yellow peppers |
| 4–6 | cloves garlic, sliced |
| 1 | tablespoon olive oil |
| ¼ | cup Basil and Garlic Chablis Blanc |

**To make the focaccia:** Pour wine into a small bowl or a 1-pint measuring cup and heat in microwave at medium setting until warm, about 5 minutes. Pour wine into a large mixing bowl, add yeast and sugar, and let proof about 10 minutes. Add ¼ cup of the oil and gradually add flour, blending well. Knead with dough hook about 5 minutes or by hand about 15 minutes, until dough is smooth and elastic. Use some of the olive oil to coat a medium-size bowl. Place dough in bowl, turning dough until completely coated. Cover with wax paper, set in a warm place, and let rise until doubled in bulk, about 1½ hours.

Punch dough down, and divide into two equal pieces. Pat each half into an oiled 8-inch or 9-inch round cake pan. Brush each focaccia with oil, cover with wax paper, and let rise in a warm place about 30 minutes. Preheat oven to 400°F. Brush each focaccia with oil again, and bake about 20 minutes, or until slightly brown.

**To prepare sautéed peppers:** While focaccia is baking, core, seed, and wash peppers. Slice lengthwise into 1-inch strips. In a large skillet over medium heat, sauté garlic in olive oil, stirring constantly, until garlic is tender but not browned. Add peppers, cover, and cook about 15 minutes, stirring occasionally, until peppers have softened. Add wine and simmer uncovered about 10 minutes. Cool slightly.

To serve, cut the focaccia into wedges and spoon the sweet peppers on top. Or slice the focaccia horizontally, spoon the peppers over the bottom piece, replace the top, and cut into wedges. Wedges can be wrapped tightly in foil and served later.

Focaccia, an Italian flatbread, can be made easily into a square or rectangular shape. Substitute square pans of equal dimension (two 8- or 9-inch pans or one 16- to 18-inch pan) or a rectangular pan (11 by 14 inches) for the round pans in this recipe.

# Caramelized Onions, Roasted Yellow Peppers, and Roasted Garlic Ricotta Pizza

*This unusual combination of ingredients blends well on pizza. You can use a favorite recipe for pizza crust, purchase a ready-made crust, or use the focaccia recipe on page 48, substituting the appropriate flavored wine and patting it into an oiled 12-inch round pan.*

## Roasted Peppers

Roasted peppers are easy to make, better-tasting, and more economical than store-bought ones. Buy red, yellow, or orange peppers in bulk when prices are low, and freeze them for later use. To freeze, slice in half from top to bottom, core, seed, rinse, and dry well with paper towels. Stack in plastic containers and freeze. Remove as needed. The peppers will lose their crunchy texture, but they can still be used in cooking for mixed salads and for roasting. Since their texture changes during freezing, the peppers will be thinner after roasting and slightly difficult to peel.

To roast peppers, place fresh or defrosted and blotted-dry pepper halves on a baking sheet, skin side up. Cook under preheated broiler until entire surface has blackened. Check every few minutes, and rearrange peppers for even roasting. Remove from baking sheet, and place in a plastic bag (sandwich or food-storage size, depending on how many peppers you have roasted). Close bag securely and set aside for 10 to 15 minutes. Remove peppers from bag one at a time. Peel skin and discard. Place peppers in a shallow rimmed dish; as they sit they will release oil. Cover tightly with plastic wrap and refrigerate. Use within 2 to 3 days.

▶ *Yield: 6–8 slices of pizza*

| | |
|---|---|
| 2 | large onions, thinly sliced |
| 1/2 | cup Sage and Roasted Garlic Chardonnay (page 15) |
| 2 | sweet yellow peppers, roasted (see box) |
| 1 | pound ricotta |
| 2 | heads roasted garlic |
| | pastry for one 12-inch pizza crust |
| | olive oil |

In a large skillet over medium heat, sauté onions in wine, stirring occasionally until tender. Increase heat to high and cook, stirring constantly, until golden brown. Set aside.

Slice roasted peppers into 1-inch strips.

In food processor, puree ricotta with roasted garlic cloves.

Preheat oven to 400°F. Place pizza crust or baked focaccia on a 12-inch round pan, brushing outer 1 inch of crust with olive oil. Spread garlic-ricotta mixture evenly over top to within 1 inch of edges. Top with roasted peppers and caramelized onions. Bake 15 to 20 minutes, until cheese is heated through and crust is golden brown. Cut into wedges.

# Savory Wine Pastry Puffs

*A well-flavored wine mixture used in the dough will produce the tastiest puffs. Larger puffs will be dense, with a more pronounced herbal wine flavor, and can be served as is. Smaller puffs are lighter and can be filled with roasted red pepper goat cheese, any of the sun-dried tomato fillings, a florentine filling, or a filling of your choice. Unfilled puffs freeze well. Place cooled puffs on a baking sheet and freeze until firm. Store in a tightly closed double plastic bag in freezer and use within 1 month. Defrost before reheating at 300°F for 10 to 15 minutes.*

▶ *Yield: 40 small (1½-inch) puffs; 30 large (2-inch) puffs*

- 1 cup Mixed Herbs and Garlic Chardonnay (page 14)
- ½ cup olive oil
- 1 cup unbleached all-purpose flour
- 4 eggs

Combine wine and olive oil in a large saucepan. Bring to a boil over medium heat. Briefly remove from heat and stir in flour. Return to flame, stirring constantly to incorporate flour, about 2 to 3 minutes. Place mixture in a mixing bowl and let cool about 2 minutes. Add eggs, one at a time, beating well after each addition.

Preheat oven to 400°F. Drop flour mixture by teaspoon, forming mounds (¾ inch wide by ¾ inch high for small puffs or 1¼ inches wide by 1¼ inches high for larger puffs) 1½ inches apart on a greased cookie sheet. Bake 12 to 15 minutes, or until slightly brown. Let cool before filling. To fill, cut off top quarter of puff with a sharp knife. Scoop out center of bottom of pastry puff and fill. Replace top.

# Onion, Green Chili, and Cheese Muffins

*Baked in mini tins, these muffins are the perfect bite-size accompaniment to chicken and meat appetizers. When prepared in a standard-size muffin tin, they are great with soups and stews. They can be made a few days ahead and reheated in the microwave. Just place four muffins at a time on a plate, cover with wax paper, and heat in the microwave at medium 2 to 3 minutes, or until heated through.*

▶ *Yield: 4 dozen mini muffins; 2 dozen standard muffins*

|     |                                                |
| --- | ---------------------------------------------- |
| 1   | tablespoon butter or margarine                 |
| 3/4 | cup Thai Pepper Chardonnay (page 16)           |
| 3/4 | cup diced onion                                |
| 3   | cups unbleached all-purpose flour              |
| 1   | teaspoon baking powder                         |
| 3/4 | cup half-and-half                              |
| 1   | can (4 ounces) diced green chili peppers       |
| 8   | ounces sharp cheddar cheese, shredded (2 cups) |

Melt butter with ¼ cup of the wine in a medium-size skillet over medium-low heat. Add onion and, stirring occasionally, sauté until tender but not browned, about 10 minutes. Set aside.

Grease muffin tins. Preheat oven to 350°F.

In a large glass mixing bowl, blend flour and baking powder with a fork. In a small bowl, mix half-and-half with remaining ½ cup wine. Add to flour mixture, blending well. Add onion mixture, chili peppers, and cheese, stirring well.

Fill muffin tins half full. Bake mini muffins 15 minutes, standard-size muffins 30 minutes, or until browned and set in the center. Cool 5 minutes before removing from tins to rack.

# Sun-Dried Tomato Pastry Swirls

*These filled pastry swirls can be prepared up to a month ahead. Just wrap tightly in a double layer of aluminum foil, and remove pieces as needed. Defrost 30 to 45 minutes before baking. You can use Neufchâtel cheese and low-fat mayonnaise for a lighter version.*

▶ *Yield: about 30 swirls*

| | |
|---|---|
| 1½ | ounces sun-dried tomatoes |
| ¼ | cup Oregano and Garlic Burgundy (page 22) |
| 12 | ounces cream cheese, softened |
| ½ | cup mayonnaise |
| 1 | package (17 ounces) frozen puff pastry sheets, defrosted |
| 1 | egg, beaten |

Reconstitute sun-dried tomatoes in wine (see box at right).

Chop tomatoes in food processor. Add cream cheese and mayonnaise and process until well blended.

Unfold 1 pastry sheet onto lightly floured pastry board. If creases are separating, lightly pat back together. Spread half of the tomato-cheese mixture over pastry to within 1 inch of edges. Roll lengthwise, ending with seam on bottom. With a sharp knife, cut into ¾-inch slices.

Preheat oven to 400°F. Place each pastry swirl on baking sheet, cut side down. Brush with egg. (Pastry swirls can be frozen at this point. Place baking sheet of pastry swirls in freezer for about 1 hour, or until frozen solid. Transfer to plastic containers, or wrap tightly in a double layer of foil. Return to freezer.) Bake 15 to 20 minutes, or until golden brown. With a spatula, immediately loosen from baking sheet. Let sit a few minutes before serving.

## Sun-Dried Tomatoes

Use sun-dried tomatoes in a dip, spread, torta, tart, or as filling for puff pastry. Reconstituted in a small amount of a wine mixture, the tomatoes absorb the flavoring, which adds a dimension of richness to their taste. Red wines, in particular, enhance the flavor of tomatoes.

To reconstitute sun-dried tomatoes, place tomatoes in a single layer in a small glass baking dish. Gently pour wine over, making sure all the tomatoes are touching liquid. Cover dish with lid or plastic wrap, and let sit at least 4 hours at room temperature. Once they have been reconstituted, the tomatoes can be stored in the refrigerator for at least 2 weeks and can be used, chopped, in salads and pasta dishes, and on pizza.

The tomatoes are also excellent, whole, in sandwiches. Place a slice of provolone or mozzarella on the bottom half of any type of crusty roll. Add several tomatoes and another slice of cheese, and replace the top of the roll. Serve as is, or heat in a 300°F oven about 10 minutes.

# Sun-Dried Tomato and Cheese Torta

*This layered cheese spread makes an attractive and delicious do-ahead party dish. It also travels well. So whether the get-together is at your place or somewhere else, be prepared for the compliments. Substitute Neufchâtel cheese and low-fat margarine to make a lighter version.*

▶ *Yield: 15–20 servings*

| | |
|---|---|
| 1½ | ounces sun-dried tomatoes |
| ¼ | cup Mixed Herb Burgundy (page 24) |
| 1 | clove garlic, crushed |
| 3 | packages (each 8 ounces) cream cheese, softened |
| 3 | cloves garlic, whole and peeled |
| ¼ | pound (1 stick) butter or margarine, softened |
| | canola oil |
| | Garnishes: chopped sun-dried tomatoes, fresh parsley or basil, chopped pignoli or walnuts |

Reconstitute sun-dried tomatoes in wine (page 53).

In a small glass bowl, mix crushed garlic with 1 package of the cream cheese. Set aside.

Finely chop tomatoes and 3 whole cloves of garlic in a food processor. Add the remaining 2 packages of cream cheese and the butter, and process until well blended.

Brush oil on the inside of a small casserole, and line with plastic wrap. Carefully spoon half of sun-dried tomato mixture into prepared casserole, and smooth to remove air bubbles. Spoon all the garlic and cream cheese mixture over sun-dried tomato mixture, spreading to cover completely the first layer of cheese torta. Top with remaining sun-dried tomato mixture. Cover with plastic wrap, and refrigerate overnight or at least 8 hours.

Unmold onto lettuce-lined serving plate. Garnish with your choice of toppings. Serve with crostini or assorted crackers.

# Sun-Dried Tomato and Spinach Tart

*A great make-ahead appetizer or main course, this was one of the first recipes developed for this book and is the only one that uses white wine in reconstituting tomatoes. Serve with a leafy green salad for a lunch or light supper entrée. A lower-fat version can be made with Neufchâtel cheese substituted for the cream cheese.*

▶ *Yield: 12–16 servings as an appetizer, 6–8 as an entrée*

|         |                                            |
|---------|--------------------------------------------|
| 1½      | ounces sun-dried tomatoes                  |
| ¼       | cup Basil Chardonnay (page 12)             |
|         | pastry for one 10-inch pie crust           |
| 1       | package (10 ounces) chopped frozen spinach |
| 2       | cloves garlic, peeled                      |
| 2       | scallions                                  |
| 2       | packages (each 8 ounces) cream cheese, softened |
| 3       | large eggs                                 |

Reconstitute sun-dried tomatoes in wine (page 53).

Preheat oven to 250°F. Roll out pie crust to fit a 9-inch or 10-inch tart pan with removable bottom. Line pan with pie crust. Bake 15 minutes, or until crust is lightly browned.

Thaw spinach according to package directions. Drain thoroughly and set aside. In food processor, chop sun-dried tomatoes, garlic, and scallions. Blend in cream cheese. Transfer to a medium-size glass bowl and stir in spinach. Add eggs, beating well after each addition.

Raise oven temperature to 300°F. Pour filling into prepared pie crust. Bake 45 minutes, or until filling is set and firm to the touch. Cool 30 minutes on a rack before unmolding.

# Sun-Dried Tomato and Roasted Garlic Cheese Spread

*Spread this on both sides of a roll for grilled chicken, smoked turkey, or roast beef sandwiches, and top with red leaf or romaine lettuce. It is also delicious on crostini: Slice a baguette into ½-inch slices and place on a baking sheet. Lightly toast in a 300°F oven about 20 minutes, turning once. For a garlic crostini, sprinkle both sides with garlic powder before baking. Make substitutions, such as Neufchâtel cheese and low-fat margarine, for a lighter version.*

▶ *Yield: about 3 cups*

|   |   |
|---|---|
| 1½ | ounces sun-dried tomatoes |
| ¼ | cup Mixed Herbs and Garlic Burgundy (page 22) |
| 1 | head (about 12 cloves) roasted garlic |
| 2 | packages (each 8 ounces) cream cheese, softened |
| ¼ | pound (1 stick) butter or margarine, softened |

Reconstitute sun-dried tomatoes in wine (page 53).

In a food processor, partially blend (do not puree) tomatoes and roasted garlic. Blend in cream cheese and butter. Can be made up to 2 days before serving. If refrigerated, bring to room temperature before serving. Transfer to serving bowl.

# Sun-Dried Tomato and Roasted Garlic Dip

*A delicious dip for raw vegetables. Substitute low-fat margarine, Neufchâtel cheese, and fat-free sour cream for a satisfying low-fat version.*

▶ *Yield: about 4 cups*

| | |
|---|---|
| 1½ | ounces sun-dried tomatoes |
| ¼ | cup Mixed Herbs and Garlic Burgundy (page 22) |
| 1 | head (about 12 cloves) roasted garlic |
| ¼ | pound (1 stick) butter or margarine, softened |
| 8 | ounces cream cheese, softened |
| 16 | ounces sour cream |

Reconstitute sun-dried tomatoes in wine (page 53).

In food processor, partially blend (do not puree) tomatoes and roasted garlic. Add butter and cream cheese, and mix until just blended. Transfer mixture to a medium-size glass bowl, and stir in sour cream until well blended. Can be made up to 2 days before serving. If refrigerated, bring to room temperature before serving. Transfer to serving bowl.

## Wine-Roasted Garlic

Make this lighter version of roasted garlic using almost any of the flavored wine mixtures. Prepare in quantity, as the garlic will keep for several weeks in the refrigerator. Use for spreads, in dips and sauces, and on pizza. Cut chilled, roasted cloves into smaller pieces, and toss into salads or vegetable and pasta dishes. To use in recipes in this book, prepare garlic with the same wine called for in the recipe.

| | |
|---|---|
| 8–10 | heads garlic |
| ¾ | cup flavored wine |

Preheat oven to 300°F. Remove the loose, papery outer layers from the heads of garlic. Place garlic upright in a 1-quart ceramic baking dish. Pour wine over garlic, and cover tightly with heavy-duty (or a double layer of) aluminum foil.

Bake for 45 to 60 minutes, basting several times, until garlic is fork-tender. Be sure to rewrap foil tightly around baking dish after each basting.

Cut off individual cloves of garlic as needed, slicing through the peel to remove the softened garlic. Garlic will firm as it cools. Use warm for spreads and when you want a creamy consistency. Chop or slice when cool. Store in the refrigerator in baking dish, covered tightly with foil.

# White Bean Dip

*This tasty dip can also be used as a spread for pita bread and bagels and can be made up to 2 days before serving.*

▶ *Yield: approximately 5 cups*

| | |
|---|---|
| 16 | ounces dried white beans |
| ½ | cup diced onion |
| 4 | cloves garlic, peeled and halved |
| 2¼ | cups Rosemary and Garlic Chardonnay (page 14) |
| 3 | cups water |
| ¼ | cup olive oil |

Pick over and rinse beans, and place in a large pot. Pour enough water over to cover by 2 inches. Bring to a boil over medium-high heat. Remove from heat, cover, and let sit 2 hours. Drain beans and rinse well. Clean pot. Place beans back in pot, adding onion and garlic. Pour 1 cup of the wine and 2 cups of the water over bean mixture. Bring to a boil over high heat, stirring occasionally. Reduce heat to low, cover, and simmer 1 hour, stirring occasionally.

Stir in 1 cup of the wine and remaining 1 cup water. Simmer until liquid has evaporated and beans are tender, 30 to 40 minutes. Let cool.

Puree bean mixture in a food processor. With processor running, add remaining ¼ cup wine and olive oil through feeder tube. Blend well. Refrigerate. Bring to room temperature before serving.

# Florentine Stuffed Mushrooms

*Spinach, prosciutto, and roasted garlic ricotta form the base of this flavorful filling. Prosciutto, an Italian ham cured in salt, is available at Italian food markets and generally available in the delicatessen section at the supermarket or specialty grocery store. If you are unable to find it, substitute smoked ham.*

*Any extra filling can be used in several ways. Stuff pita bread, brush with olive oil, and bake in a 350°F oven until pita is crisp and cheese filling is heated through. Or use as a filling for chicken breasts. Pound the chicken flat, spread the filling over, and roll up. Pour ½ cup of a wine mixture over the chicken rolls, cover loosely with foil, and bake in a 350°F oven 30 to 40 minutes.*

▶ *Yield: 6–8 servings*

| | |
|---|---|
| ¼ | cup onion, diced |
| 1 | cup Parsley and Garlic Chablis Blanc (page 16) |
| 1 | package (10 ounces) frozen chopped spinach, defrosted and drained well |
| 1 | pound ricotta |
| 4–6 | cloves roasted garlic |
| ¼ | pound prosciutto, chopped |
| | freshly ground black pepper |
| 2 | pounds large mushrooms, stems removed and wiped clean |
| 1 | tablespoon butter or margarine |

Sauté onion in ¼ cup of the wine in a medium-size skillet over medium heat until liquid has evaporated. Reduce heat to low, add spinach, and cook for a few minutes, stirring well. Remove from heat.

In a food processor, puree ricotta and roasted garlic. Blend pureed cheese mixture, spinach, and prosciutto in a large mixing bowl. Add pepper to taste.

Preheat oven to 350°F. Place mushrooms, cavity side up, in a medium-size glass baking dish. Spoon filling into the cavity of each mushroom. Melt butter in a small saucepan over medium heat. Add remaining wine andblend well. Spoon a teaspoonful of sauce over each stuffed mushroom, and pour remaining sauce around bottom of baking dish. Cover loosely with foil. Bake about 35 minutes.

# Baked Stuffed Clams

*As a hearty appetizer or as a satisfying dinner served with a salad, this seasoned clam filling can be made several hours ahead. Store in a glass or ceramic bowl, cover tightly with plastic wrap, and refrigerate until ready to assemble. Use 4½-inch or 5-inch natural baking shells for filling. They are available at most kitchen accessory shops.*

▶ *Yield: 4–6 servings*

|        |                                                      |
|--------|------------------------------------------------------|
| 1      | tablespoon butter or margarine                       |
| ⅔–1    | cup Oregano, Fennel, and Garlic Chardonnay (page 15) |
| ¼      | cup chopped onion                                    |
| 1      | stalk celery, diced                                  |
| 2      | cans (each 6½ ounces) minced clams, undrained        |
| 2      | cloves garlic, crushed                               |
| 1      | tablespoon chopped fresh parsley                     |
| 1½     | cups flavored bread crumbs (page 38)                 |
| ½      | cup grated Parmesan                                   |
| 6      | natural baking shells                                |
|        | butter or margarine                                  |

Melt 1 tablespoon butter in a medium-size skillet over medium heat. Blend in ⅓ cup of the wine. Add onion and celery. Sauté, stirring occasionally, until vegetables are fork-tender, about 15 minutes.

In a large mixing bowl, combine clams and clam juice, garlic, and parsley, mixing well. Add bread crumbs, the remaining ⅓ cup wine, the onion-celery mixture, and ¼ cup of the cheese. Mixture should be slightly moist. If too dry, add more wine.

Preheat oven to 350°F. Lightly grease baking shells and place on a baking sheet. Divide mixture, filling each shell equally. Dot each with butter and sprinkle with remaining cheese. Bake 15 to 20 minutes or until heated through.

# Ricotta Salata Crostini

*Use only the best ingredients for this incredibly delicious, yet easy and versatile appetizer. Ricotta salata is a cross in taste and texture between feta and goat cheese. It is usually available in the specialty cheese department of supermarkets. If you cannot find it, substitute a combination of equal parts feta and goat cheese, blended and spread on top of crostini. Directions are provided for a warm and cold version of this recipe.*

▶ *Yield: 8–10 slices*

| | |
|---|---|
| ¼ | cup Basil, Parsley, and Garlic Burgundy (page 23) |
| ¼ | cup olive oil |
| ½ | teaspoon freshly ground black pepper |
| 1 | loaf (1 pound) crusty bread, cut into ¾-inch slices |
| ½ | pound ricotta salata, thinly sliced to equal bread slices |

In a small bowl, thoroughly mix wine, olive oil, and pepper with a fork or whisk.

Preheat oven to 350°F. Place sliced bread on baking sheet. Bake 10 to 15 minutes, turning bread once until both sides are slightly crisp. Remove from oven and increase temperature to 400°F. Working quickly, spoon ½ to 1 tablespoon of the wine-and-oil mixture over tops of bread, spreading to edges. Top with a slice of cheese. Bake 5 to 10 minutes until cheese is warm.

To serve cold, spread wine-and-oil mixture on unheated bread. Top with cheese and serve.

# Tomato and Shrimp Gazpacho with Roasted Garlic Sour Cream

*When first made, this flavorful soup has a fresh cucumber tang. Let the flavors blend overnight for a rich, mellow taste. For a heartier soup, add more shrimp. The roasted garlic sour cream is easily made in advance and can also be used as a topping for baked potatoes and many Mexican dishes.*

▶ *Yield: 4–6 servings*

| | |
|---|---|
| ½ | cup Chervil and Marjoram Rosé (page 28) |
| 1 | tablespoon olive oil |
| 2 | cloves garlic, peeled |
| 6 | medium ripe tomatoes, peeled |
| 1 | large cucumber, peeled |
| ½ | red onion |
| ½ | sweet green pepper, cored and seeded |
| 3 | cloves roasted garlic |
| 1 | cup sour cream |
| ½ | pound cooked large shrimp, peeled and deveined |
| 2 | tablespoons chopped fresh chervil (optional) |

In food processor, blend wine, olive oil, and garlic.

Cut tomatoes, cucumber, onion, and green pepper to fit feed tube of processor. Using a pulse motion, add vegetable pieces one at a time until mixture is smooth. Transfer to bowl, cover with plastic wrap, and store in refrigerator until ready to serve.

To prepare roasted garlic sour cream, mash roasted garlic with a fork in a small glass bowl. Blend in sour cream. Store in refrigerator until ready to use.

Just before serving, reserve 4 to 6 shrimp for garnish and cut the remaining shrimp into bite-size pieces. Divide chopped shrimp among the soup bowls. Spoon gazpacho over shrimp. Top with roasted garlic sour cream, and garnish with a whole shrimp. Sprinkle fresh chervil over sour cream and shrimp, if desired.

# Red Berry Soup

*Great for a spring or summer brunch, lunch, or dinner, this refreshing chilled fruit soup can be made a day ahead.*

▶ *Yield: 4 servings*

> 12 ounces frozen strawberries (not in syrup), defrosted
> 1/2 cup marinated raspberries from Raspberry Chardonnay
> 1/2 cup Raspberry Chardonnay (page 13)
> 1 tablespoon sugar
> 1/2 cup half-and-half

In food processor, puree strawberries and raspberries.

Bring wine and sugar to a boil in a small saucepan over medium-high heat. Boil, stirring constantly, 1 minute. Remove from heat and cool for a few minutes. Slowly stir in half-and-half. Return to heat, bring to a boil, and cook, stirring constantly, 1 minute. Remove from heat and let cool about 5 minutes.

Add cooked mixture to berries in food processor. Blend well. Transfer to a glass bowl, cover with plastic wrap, and refrigerate for at least 2 hours before serving.

# Broccoli Soup

*With an unusual creamy-crunchy texture, this broccoli soup can be served hot, cold, or at room temperature. Reheating provides a more flavorful soup. Use only fresh broccoli to prepare this soup.*

▶ *Yield: 4 servings*

> 1 pound fresh broccoli florets, washed and drained
> 3/4 cup Parsley and Garlic Chablis Blanc (page 16)
> 1/2 cup onion, coarsely chopped
> 1 clove garlic, peeled
> 1 cup half-and-half

Place broccoli florets in a medium casserole; pour 1/2 cup of the wine over. Cover with wax paper and cook at medium high in microwave 3 minutes. Set aside until cool.

Place broccoli and cooking liquid in a food processor, add onion and garlic, and puree to a very fine texture. Combine half-and-half with remaining 1/4 cup wine. With processor running, slowly pour through feed tube and process until well blended.

# Potato and Cauliflower Soup with Scallions

*A creamy soup that can be served hot or cold.*

▶ *Yield: 4–6 servings*

    1   package (10 ounces) frozen cauliflower florets
 1¾  cups Chervil, Chive, and Dill Rhine Wine (page 20)
    1   small onion, diced
    1   tablespoon butter or margarine
    2   medium potatoes, cooked, peeled, and quartered
  ¾  cup half-and-half
  ½  cup chopped scallions
  ½  teaspoon freshly ground black pepper

Place frozen cauliflower in a small casserole, and pour ¼ cup of the wine over. Cover with wax paper and cook in the microwave at medium-high about 6 minutes or until tender, stirring halfway through cooking time. Cool. In a medium-size skillet, sauté onion in butter over medium heat until tender, about 10 minutes. Cool slightly.

Puree cauliflower mixture, sautéed onion, and potatoes in food processor. Slowly add half-and-half. Transfer to a medium-size bowl and cover with plastic wrap. Chill, if serving cold; or, heat in the microwave at medium about 4 minutes, stirring once during cooking process.

Just before serving, stir in ¼ cup of the chopped scallions and black pepper. Spoon into soup dishes. Top with remaining scallions.

# Vegetable Soup with Roasted Garlic Bread

*This tasty soup, served with the vegetables or strained and served as a broth, can be made earlier in the day and reheated. The roasted garlic bread can also be prepared ahead of time and kept loosely wrapped in foil until ready to use.*

▶ *Yield: 4 servings*

|   |   |
|---|---|
| 1 | large tomato, peeled and cut into 1-inch pieces |
| 1 | small onion, chopped |
| 1 | carrot, peeled and sliced thin |
| 1 | medium zucchini, peeled and diced |
| 1 | stalk celery, sliced |
| ½ | cup yellow celery leaves |
| 2 | cloves garlic, peeled and sliced |
| 3 | tablespoons olive oil |
| 2 | cups water |
| 1 | cup Basil, Parsley, and Garlic Burgundy (page 23) |
| 1 | head roasted garlic |
| 4 | slices (1 inch thick) crusty bread, toasted on both sides |

In a large saucepan over medium heat, sauté tomato, onion, carrot, zucchini, celery, celery leaves, and sliced garlic in olive oil about 10 minutes, stirring often. Stir in water and wine. Simmer, partially covered, stirring occasionally, about 45 minutes.

Spread roasted garlic on toasted bread. Place one slice in bottom of each soup bowl and spoon soup over bread. Serve immediately.

This roasted garlic bread is similar to bruschetta, which consists of thick bread slices that are grilled and drizzled with oil. For a lighter version, make crostini. Cut a baguette into ½-inch-thick slices and toast both sides. Both bruschetta and crostini can be made up to 24 hours before serving.

# Bean and Spinach Soup

*This soup is very thick. For a thinner consistency, add ½ cup wine and ½ cup water after soup starts to boil, just before serving.*

▶ *Yield: 6–8 servings*

| | |
|---|---|
| 1 | package (16 ounces) dried red kidney beans |
| 2 | packages (each 10 ounces) frozen chopped spinach |
| 3 | cloves garlic, peeled and sliced |
| ¼ | cup olive oil |
| ¼ | cup chopped fresh parsley |
| 2 | cups Parsley, Chive, and Garlic Rhine Wine (page 19) |
| 2 | cups water |

Pick over beans and rinse well. Place in a large saucepan. Pour water over beans to cover by 2 inches. Bring to a boil over high heat. Remove from heat, cover, and let sit 2 hours. Drain, rinse, and drain again. Return beans to clean saucepan and cover with water. Bring to a boil over high heat. Reduce heat to low, and simmer 30 minutes, stirring occasionally. Rinse and drain.

Prepare spinach according to package directions. Drain thoroughly. In a large, clean saucepan, sauté garlic and spinach in olive oil over medium heat about 5 minutes, or until heated through. Do not brown garlic. Stir in parsley, beans, wine, and 2 cups of water. Cook, stirring occasionally, until mixture starts to boil. Remove from heat and serve.

# Chapter Eight

# Salads, Marinades, Sauces, and Relishes

*One cannot think well, love well, sleep well,*
*if one has not dined well.*

— Virginia Woolf

For salads, marinades, sauces, and relishes, the condiments used in the dressing are what enhance the completed dish. A mellow wine flavored with herbs, spices, vegetables, or fruits adds an extra degree of flavor.

In a salad, the flavored wine imparts its essence, highlighting each ingredient while blending them all together. Flavored wine in marinades seasons as it tenderizes, with the flavor absorbed while marinating and cooking.

Almost any liquid in a sauce can be replaced by a flavored wine, which will infuse the sauce with its delicate seasonings. Relishes benefit more so. Since the vegetables or fruits in the relishes absorb the flavored wine, they are more substantial than a sauce.

# Greek Potato Salad

*Feta cheese and spinach offer a new twist to potato salad. Prepare this dish earlier in the day and keep refrigerated. Serve at room temperature.*

▶ *Yield: 6–8 servings*

|   |   |
|---|---|
| 1/2 | cup Thyme, Tarragon, and Chive Cabernet Sauvignon (page 26) |
| 1/4 | cup olive oil |
| 2 | pounds white potatoes, peeled, cooked, and cut into 1-inch cubes |
| 1/2 | cup chopped scallions |
| 4 | ounces fresh spinach leaves, washed and drained |
| 1 | roasted red pepper, cut into thin strips (page 50) |
| 4 | ounces feta cheese, crumbled |
|   | freshly ground black pepper |

In a small bowl, combine wine and olive oil, blending well with a fork. In a medium-size glass bowl, stir warm, cooked potatoes with scallions. Pour wine-and-oil mixture over, and stir well. Add spinach, red pepper, and feta cheese. Toss gently to mix. Sprinkle with black pepper to taste.

## Choosing and Preparing Spinach

When purchasing fresh spinach in a bag, check the leaves for excessive browning. Whether using fresh from the garden or bagged, for best results, remove most of the stem that runs up the center of the leaf. Spinach leaves must be thoroughly washed and dried before using, as bits of soil can become embedded in the leaves.

# Panzanella

*Use the freshest, ripest tomatoes and a loaf of good-quality crusty bread for this delicious Italian tomato and bread salad. Add the bread just before serving.*

▶ *Yield: 4–8 servings*

| | |
|---|---|
| ½ | cup Basil, Parsley, and Garlic Burgundy (page 23) |
| ¼ | cup olive oil |
| 2 | cloves garlic, peeled and crushed |
| 6 | large tomatoes, cut into wedges |
| ½ | red onion, sliced, then chopped into 1-inch pieces |
| 8 | ounces crusty bread, cut into 1-inch cubes |
| | freshly ground black pepper |
| 2 | tablespoons chopped fresh basil (optional) |

In a small bowl, blend wine, oil, and garlic with a fork. In a medium-size glass bowl, toss tomatoes with red onion; pour wine mixture over. When ready to serve, lightly toss in bread cubes. Add pepper to taste. Sprinkle with fresh basil, if desired. Serve immediately.

# Ham and Vegetable Salad

*Though delicious with smoked or honey ham, you can substitute diced, cooked chicken or turkey. The cheese is optional. This also makes a great filling for pita bread.*

▶ *Yield: 4 servings*

| | |
|---|---|
| ¼ | cup Sage and Roasted Garlic Chardonnay (page 15) |
| ¼ | cup olive oil |
| ½ | teaspoon Dijon mustard |
| | freshly ground black pepper |
| 1 | cup diced smoked or honey ham |
| 2 | roma tomatoes, chopped into 1-inch pieces |
| ½ | cup fresh broccoli florets, chopped |
| ⅓ | cup diced sweet green pepper |
| ¼ | cup chopped scallions |
| ½ | cup shredded cheddar cheese |

In a small bowl, thoroughly mix wine, olive oil, mustard, and black pepper with a fork.

In a medium-size glass bowl, combine ham, tomatoes, broccoli, green pepper, scallions, and cheese. Pour dressing over ham and vegetables. Serve at room temperature. Toss before serving.

# Broccoli Salad

*Parmesan cheese in the dressing enhances this salad.*

▶ *Yield: 4 servings*

| | |
|---|---|
| ¼ | cup plus 1 tablespoon Basil and Garlic Rosé (page 29) |
| ¼ | cup olive oil |
| 1 | tablespoon grated Parmesan |
| ½ | teaspoon freshly ground black pepper |
| 1 | pound fresh broccoli florets, rinsed and drained |
| ½ | red onion, chopped |

To make dressing, combine wine, olive oil, cheese, and pepper in a small bowl, mixing well with a fork. Place broccoli and onion in a medium-size glass bowl and toss lightly. Pour dressing over broccoli and onion. Cover with plastic wrap and refrigerate. Let sit at least 1 hour before serving at room temperature, mixing well before serving.

# Checkerboard Pasta Salad

*This pasta salad gets its name from the black olives and red peppers. If rotini or radiatore pasta is not available, substitute rigatoni or ziti.*

▶ *Yield: 4 servings*

| | |
|---|---|
| ½ | cup Parsley and Savory Rosé (page 29) |
| ¼ | cup plus 1 tablespoon olive oil |
| ½ | teaspoon freshly ground black pepper |
| 1 | pound rotini or radiatore pasta |
| 1 | sweet red pepper, diced |
| 2 | cans (each 8 ounces) sliced black olives, drained |
| | grated Parmesan |
| 2 | tablespoons chopped fresh Italian parsley (optional) |

In a small bowl, blend wine, ¼ cup of the olive oil, and black pepper with a fork. Prepare pasta according to package directions. Drain, rinse, and drain again.

In a medium-size glass bowl, toss pasta with remaining 1 tablespoon olive oil to coat. Add red pepper and olives, and mix well. Pour dressing over pasta mixture. Let sit, refrigerated, at least 2 hours, stirring well several times. Serve at room temperature. Sprinkle with cheese and Italian parsley, if desired, before serving. Toss lightly.

# Green Beans and Mushroom Salad

*Crunchy fresh green beans and fresh mushrooms provide an unusual combination of textures in this salad.*

▶ *Yield: 4–6 servings*

- ½  cup Sage and Garlic Rosé (page 28)
- ¼  cup olive oil
- 2  cloves garlic, finely chopped
- 1  pound fresh green beans, rinsed, drained, and cut diagonally into 1-inch pieces
- 8  ounces mushrooms, cleaned and sliced
- 1  tablespoon chopped fresh sage (optional)

In a small bowl, mix wine, olive oil, and garlic with a fork until thoroughly blended. Combine beans and mushrooms in a medium-size glass bowl. Pour wine mixture over, and stir well to coat. Cover with plastic wrap and refrigerate. Bring to room temperature, add fresh sage, if desired, and toss before serving.

# Bow-Tie Pasta Salad

*Although this recipe calls for bow-tie pasta, fuselli or rotini will work just as well.*

▶ *Yield: 4 servings*

- ½  cup Parsley and Savory Merlot (page 24)
- ⅓  cup plus 1 tablespoon olive oil
- 2  cloves garlic, crushed
- ½  teaspoon freshly ground black pepper
- 12  ounces bow-tie pasta
- 4  roma tomatoes, chopped
- 1  sweet green pepper, diced
- 2  tablespoons chopped fresh parsley

In a small bowl, combine wine, ⅓ cup olive oil, garlic, and black pepper with a fork until thoroughly blended. Cook bow-tie pasta according to package directions. Drain, rinse, and drain again.

In a medium-size glass bowl, toss remaining 1 tablespoon oil with pasta to coat. Add tomatoes, green pepper, and parsley. Mix well. Pour dressing over, stirring well. Refrigerate and let sit at least 2 hours, stirring several times. Mix well and serve at room temperature.

# Black Bean, Tomato, and Onion Salad

*The Chili Pepper Cabernet Sauvignon adds a "kick" to this salad. For a tamer version, use another herbal wine mixture. The dried beans give this salad a crunchy texture, but if you prefer, you can substitute drained canned beans for the dried.*

▶ *Yield: 6–8 servings*

|   |   |
|---|---|
| 8 | ounces dried black beans |
| 1/2 | cup Chili Pepper Cabernet Sauvignon (page 27) |
| 1/2 | cup olive oil |
| 2 | cloves garlic, crushed |
| 1 | small red onion, chopped |
| 4 | tomatoes, cut into 1-inch pieces |

Pick over and rinse beans. Place beans in a medium-size saucepan, cover with 2 inches of water, and bring to a boil. Boil for 5 minutes, remove from heat, cover, and let sit for 1 hour. Drain and rinse. Return beans to clean saucepan, cover with water, and bring to a second boil. Remove from heat, cover, and let sit 30 minutes. Drain, rinse, and drain again.

In a small bowl, blend wine, olive oil, and garlic with a fork. Place beans in a medium-size casserole. Pour half of the dressing over beans. Layer onion over beans, then top with tomatoes. Pour remaining dressing over tomatoes. Cover and let sit, refrigerated, for at least 2 hours. Toss well before serving.

# Spinach Salad

*This salad can be served as a side dish or as an entrée.*

▶ *Yield: 4 servings as a side dish, 2 as an entrée*

|   |   |
|---|---|
| 4 | cups fresh spinach leaves, rinsed and drained |
| 1/2 | cup thinly sliced red onion |
| 3 | hard-cooked eggs, coarsely chopped |
| 1/2 | cup crumbled cooked bacon |
| 1/2 | cup Basil, Fennel, and Garlic Rosé (page 30) |
| 1/2 | cup olive oil |
| 1 | teaspoon Dijon mustard |

Pat spinach leaves with paper towels to remove all moisture. Tear into bite-size pieces and place in a large bowl. Add onion, eggs, and bacon, and toss gently to mix.

In a mini processor, mix wine, olive oil, and mustard until well blended. Pour over spinach salad, and toss to coat. Serve immediately.

# Chicken Salad with Sun-Dried Tomatoes, Scallions, and Parsley

*Make a double batch of this recipe and use it, heated, as a filling for crepes and pastry shells. To heat, place the salad in a casserole dish, cover with wax paper, and microwave at medium about 3 to 4 minutes. Spoon into crepes or shells.*

▶ *Yield: 2–3 servings*

| | |
|---|---|
| 1½ | ounces sun-dried tomatoes |
| ¾ | cup plus 2 tablespoons Parsley and Garlic Chablis Blanc (page 16) |
| 2 | quarts water |
| 1 | pound skinless, boneless chicken breasts |
| ¼ | cup chopped scallions |
| ¼ | cup plus 1 tablespoon chopped fresh parsley |
| ½ | cup mayonnaise |

Reconstitute sun-dried tomatoes in ¼ cup of the wine (page 53). Chop tomatoes to make ⅓ cup.

Pour water and ½ cup of the wine into a large pot. Add chicken. Over low heat, gently simmer about 15 to 20 minutes, or until chicken is cooked through. Remove to platter and let cool.

Cut chicken into bite-size pieces, and place in a medium-size glass bowl. Add tomatoes, scallions, and ¼ cup parsley, and toss to mix well.

In a small bowl, mix mayonnaise with remaining 2 tablespoons wine. Stir in 1 tablespoon parsley. Pour over chicken mixture; toss to coat.

# Marinades

Marinades add flavor while tenderizing and moisturizing. The base can be made with any combination of oil and an acid-based liquid such as vinegar or wine. Since vinegar is tart and very acidic, wine seems to be the perfect natural alternative when preparing marinades. Any marinade calling for vinegar can be replaced with a flavored wine mixture.

The easiest method for preparing marinades requires a glass measuring cup and a fork. In most cases, you can measure the ingredients right in the measuring cup, blend, and store until ready to use. Using a fork when mixing helps to emulsify the oil, providing a better blend of ingredients. Most marinades can be made ahead, allowing the flavors to meld.

Foods should be marinated for at least several hours and, depending on the food, can be marinated overnight. Always use a glass or ceramic baking dish, and cover tightly with plastic wrap. If marinating overnight in the refrigerator, the food should be turned several times in the marinade. Bring food to room temperature before cooking.

The recipes that follow will give you a start in preparing your own "special blend" of marinades. All varieties of white, red, and rosé wine can be used. Additions can include mustard, honey, lemon juice, sesame seed oil, soy sauce, garlic, fresh pepper, and various seeds, such as caraway, dill, and fennel. Just remember to keep the condiments compatible with the flavoring of the wine mixture.

## Which Wine?

As a general rule, use white wine for light-colored foods, such as chicken and white fish; rosé for medium-colored foods, such as pork, and when the cooking method or sauce will add color to a light-colored food; and red wine for darker foods, such as beef and certain kinds of fish.

# Orange Mango Chardonnay Marinade

*Use for chicken. After marinating, sauté, broil, or grill chicken. Top with an orange mango salsa.*

▶ *Yield: 1 cup*

    $3/4$   cup Orange Mango Chardonnay (page 13)
    $1/4$   cup canola oil
    $1/4$   teaspoon cayenne
    $1/8$   teaspoon nutmeg

Thoroughly blend all ingredients with a fork in a glass measuring cup.


# Italian Herb Chardonnay Marinade

*A versatile marinade for beef, chicken, pork, or fish.*

▶ *Yield: $3/4$ cup*

    $1/2$   cup Italian Herb Chardonnay (page 15)
    3   tablespoons olive oil
    2   cloves garlic, crushed
    1   tablespoon lemon juice
    1   teaspoon freshly ground black pepper

Thoroughly blend all ingredients with a fork in a glass measuring cup.


# Sage and Roasted Garlic Chardonnay Marinade

*This is excellent with pork, chicken, or beef.*

▶ *Yield: about 1 cup*

    $1/2$   cup Sage and Roasted Garlic Chardonnay (page 15)
    4   cloves roasted garlic, mashed
    2   tablespoons soy sauce
    1   tablespoon honey

Thoroughly blend all ingredients with a fork in a glass measuring cup.

# Parsley and Garlic Rosé Marinade

*Use with fish, pork, chicken, or beef.*

▶ *Yield: ¾ cup*

- ½ cup Parsley and Garlic Rosé (page 28)
- 3 tablespoons canola oil
- 1 tablespoon soy sauce
- 2 cloves garlic, crushed

Thoroughly blend all ingredients with a fork in a glass measuring cup.

# Rosemary and Black Peppercorn Rosé Marinade

*A tangy marinade that is good with pork and beef.*

▶ *Yield: 1 cup*

- ½ cup Rosemary and Black Peppercorn Rosé (page 30)
- ½ cup olive oil
- 1 tablespoon fresh whole black peppercorns (not from wine mixture)

Thoroughly blend wine and olive oil with a fork in a glass measuring cup. Stir in peppercorns.

# Garlic and Chive Burgundy Marinade

*Great with beef and pork.*

▶ *Yield: ¾ cup*

- ½ cup Garlic and Chive Burgundy (page 22)
- 2 tablespoons canola oil
- 1 tablespoon sesame seed oil
- 1 clove garlic, crushed

Thoroughly blend all ingredients with a fork in a glass measuring cup.

# Rosemary and Garlic Burgundy Marinade

*Use with beef.*

▶ *Yield: ¾ cup*

    ½   cup Rosemary and Garlic Burgundy (page 23)
    3   tablespoons olive oil
    1   tablespoon lemon juice
    1   teaspoon freshly ground black pepper

Thoroughly blend all ingredients with a fork in a glass measuring cup.


# Parsley and Savory Merlot Marinade

*Use in Stuffed Marinated Flank Steak (page 120), or for other beef dishes.*

▶ *Yield: about 1 cup*

    ½   cup Parsley and Savory Merlot (page 24)
    ¼   cup olive oil
    1   tablespoon Dijon mustard
    2   cloves garlic, crushed
    ½   teaspoon freshly ground black pepper

Thoroughly blend all ingredients with a fork in a glass measuring cup.

## Sauces

Sauces are an essential part of many of the recipes in this book. The following are variations on basic sauces. By using different flavored wine mixtures, you can have an unlimited collection of recipes that can customize any dish you prepare. You can substitute low-fat margarine in the Basic Wine Sauce and the Mushroom Sauce.

## Mushroom Sauce

*In addition to the button mushrooms that are readily available, you can use any of the specialty mushrooms, especially the cremini or portobello.*

▶ *Yield: about 1 cup*

    2  tablespoons butter or margarine
    8  ounces mushrooms, sliced or chopped
  3/4  cup flavored wine mixture

Melt butter in a small saucepan over medium heat. Add mushrooms, and cook, stirring often, until tender, about 10 minutes. Stir in wine, and cook until heated through.

## Light Béchamel Sauce

*This exceptional sauce substitutes a small amount of half-and-half and flavored wine for the cream in the classic version of béchamel.*

▶ *Yield: 2 cups*

    2  tablespoons butter or margarine
    2  tablespoons unbleached all-purpose flour
  1/4  cup half-and-half
 13/4  cups Basil, Fennel, and Garlic Chablis Blanc (page 18)

Melt butter in a medium-size saucepan over low heat. Blend in flour, stirring well.

Mix half-and-half and wine in a 1-quart measuring cup. Slowly stir into flour mixture, stirring until sauce has thickened. If sauce becomes too thick, thin with a little more wine.

# Basic Wine Sauce

*Use for chicken, fish, and vegetable dishes.*

▶ *Yield: ½ cup*

    2   tablespoons butter or margarine
    ½   cup flavored wine mixture

Melt butter in a small saucepan over medium heat. Stir in wine until thoroughly blended and sauce is heated through.

# Basic Tomato Sauce

*Excellent on pizza and with pasta.*

▶ *Yield: about 3 cups*

    2–3   cloves garlic, crushed
    1     tablespoon olive oil
    1     can (28 ounces) good-quality crushed tomatoes
    ¼     cup Rosemary and Garlic Burgundy (page 23)

In a medium-size saucepan over medium heat, sauté garlic in olive oil until tender but not browned, about 5 minutes. Slowly add crushed tomatoes, reduce heat to low, and simmer about 20 minutes, until slightly thick. Stir in wine; simmer about 10 minutes more.

# Fresh Tomato Sauce

*Try this flavorful, rich sauce with any cheese-filled pasta.*

▶ *Yield: about 1 cup*

    2   cloves garlic, sliced thin
    2   tablespoons olive oil
    3   large tomatoes, peeled and chopped
    ¼   cup Basil, Fennel, and Garlic Rosé (page 30)

In a medium-size skillet over low heat, sauté garlic in olive oil until tender but not browned, about 5 minutes. Add tomatoes, then increase heat to medium high. Cook 10 to 15 minutes, stirring often, until liquid is reduced by half and sauce has thickened. Reduce heat to low and add wine. Let simmer about 10 minutes, stirring occasionally.

# Burgundy Tomato and Roasted Garlic Sauce

*An intensified version of the Basic Tomato Sauce. Use for pasta, beef, and pizza.*

▶ *Yield: about 3 cups*

> $1/4$   cup olive oil
> 8   cloves roasted garlic
> 1   can (28 ounces) good-quality crushed tomatoes
> $1/2$   cup Oregano and Garlic Burgundy (page 22)

Heat olive oil in a medium-size saucepan over low heat until warm. Add roasted garlic, and crush, blending well with oil. Cook about 3 minutes. Add crushed tomatoes, cooking over low heat until sauce starts to boil. Pour in wine, stirring occasionally, until sauce is heated through and is of desired consistency; the longer the sauce cooks, the thicker it will become.

# Red Pesto Sauce

*Excellent with pasta and chicken, as a spread on sandwiches, and as a topping for crostini.*

▶ *Yield: about 1½ cups*

> $1^{1}/2$   ounces sun-dried tomatoes
> $1/2$   cup Double Red Pepper Rosé (page 31)
> 2   large roasted red peppers (page 50)
> 3   cloves garlic, peeled
> $1/2$   cup pine nuts, toasted
> $1/3$   cup grated Parmesan
> 2   tablespoons olive oil

Reconstitute tomatoes using ¼ cup of the wine (page 53).

In a food processor, coarsely chop tomatoes, roasted peppers, and garlic. Blend in pine nuts and cheese. With processor running, pour in olive oil and remaining wine until sauce just binds.

Store in refrigerator, covered with olive oil. Use within 5 days.

# Relishes

These savory relishes are not traditional, since they do not require preserving. Stored in the refrigerator in a glass bowl covered with plastic wrap, they will keep for up to 2 weeks. Use as a garnish on beef, pork, chicken, or fish and as a spread on sandwiches.❧

## Onion and Brown Sugar Relish

*This sweet relish is great on pork, chicken, or hamburgers. It also makes a nice topping for mashed potatoes and can be mixed into stuffing.*

▶ *Yield: about 1½ cups*

>     3   large onions, quartered
>     2   tablespoons olive oil
>    ¼    cup Coriander and Peppercorn Rhine Wine (page 20)
>    ¼    cup dark brown sugar

Finely chop onions in food processor.

Warm olive oil and wine in a large skillet over medium-low heat. Add onions, and cook, stirring occasionally, until onions are tender, about 10 to 15 minutes. Stir in brown sugar until sugar has dissolved and color of relish is even.

# Roma Tomato and Onion Relish

*A very rich, dense relish. Spread on focaccia or crostini, top with sliced provolone or mozzarella, and bake until cheese is slightly melted.*

▶ *Yield: about 3 cups*

2   pounds roma tomatoes
6   cloves garlic, peeled
1   cup Garlic and Chive Burgundy (page 22)
1   medium onion, chopped

In a food processor, coarsely chop tomatoes and garlic.

Pour ½ cup of the wine into a large skillet, and warm over medium heat. Add tomato and garlic mixture, and simmer, stirring occasionally, about 30 minutes, until liquid is reduced by half.

Add onion and remaining ½ cup wine. Simmer about 15 minutes, stirring often, until liquid is reduced and relish is very thick. Can be used hot or cold.

# Chapter Nine

# Pasta, Grains, Beans, and Eggs

*If pale beans bubble for you in a red earthenware pot,*
*You can oft decline the dinners of sumptuous hosts.*

— Marcus Valerius Martialis

Each pasta dish in this chapter is a satisfying entrée. Although the Lasagne Bundles is the only recipe that calls for cooking the noodles in a wine-and-water mixture, any other pasta can also be cooked in a flavored wine (see page 85).

Grains and beans also utilize flavored wine, allowing the wine to infuse the food with its flavor while absorbing the cooking liquid.

The egg-based recipes benefit from flavored wines as well. The wines are used in batters and fillings, for cooking ingredients added to the eggs, and to season a delicate, yet hearty, soufflé. 🍇

# Ravioli with Broccoli

*Double Red Pepper Chablis Blanc adds spice to this dish. For a more traditional flavor, use Basil, Fennel, and Garlic Chablis Blanc. This reheats well in the microwave: Cook at medium heat, covered with wax paper, about 5 minutes, or until heated through; toss before serving.*

▶ *Yield: 3–4 servings*

```
4    cloves garlic, sliced
4    tablespoons olive oil
1/2  pound fresh broccoli florets, rinsed and drained
1    cup Double Red Pepper Chablis Blanc (page 16)
1    pound frozen mini ravioli
1/3  cup chopped roasted red pepper (page 50)
     grated Parmesan
```

Boil water for ravioli.

In a medium-size skillet over medium heat, sauté garlic in 2 tablespoons of the olive oil until the garlic starts to turn golden brown. Immediately reduce heat to low and stir in broccoli to coat with oil. Pour wine over broccoli and garlic, cover, and simmer 10 to 15 minutes, or until broccoli is tender. Stir in remaining 2 tablespoons of olive oil.

Place ravioli in boiling water and cook according to package directions. Drain, rinse, and drain again. Add ravioli to broccoli mixture in skillet. Stir in roasted red pepper and toss to mix well. Spoon onto serving plates and top with grated Parmesan cheese.

# Fettuccine with Shrimp and Artichoke Sauce

*A quick and delicious meal, this fettuccine is topped with a shrimp and artichoke white-wine cream sauce flavored with tangy lemon.*

▶ *Yield: 4 servings*

| | |
|---|---|
| ½ | pound fettuccine |
| 2 | tablespoons butter or margarine |
| ¼ | cup unbleached all-purpose flour |
| 1½ | cups Basil and Garlic Chablis Blanc (page 17) |
| 2 | teaspoons lemon juice |
| 1 | pound cooked medium shrimp, peeled and deveined |
| 1 | can (14 ounces) artichokes, drained and cut into quarters |
| | freshly ground black pepper |
| 1 | tablespoon chopped fresh basil (optional) |

Prepare fettuccine according to package directions.

In a medium-size saucepan over medium heat, melt butter. Add flour to make a roux, stirring well to blend butter and flour. Slowly stir in wine, ½ cup at a time, and blend thoroughly after each addition. Stir in lemon juice, shrimp, and artichokes. Add pepper to taste.

Divide fettuccine among four plates. Spoon sauce over. Sprinkle with fresh basil, if desired. Serve immediately.

## Flavoring Pasta

To add a subtle flavor to unflavored pasta, cook it in a wine-and-water mixture. Add about 1 cup of flavored wine to 1 quart of water before bringing to a boil. Use more or less to taste.

# Lasagne Bundles

*Cooking the lasagne noodles in a skillet with wine infuses the pasta with flavor. Although this method does take a little extra time, the results are worth it. Fortunately, this dish can be prepared up to a day ahead, then reheated in the microwave: Cover with wax paper, and cook at medium power about 10 minutes, turning once during cooking. Serve with Fresh Tomato Sauce and Light Béchamel Sauce.*

▶ *Yield: 4–6 servings*

| | |
|---|---|
| 1 pound ricotta | 1½ cups water |
| 1 egg | 8 lasagne noodles |
| 1 tablespoon parsley flakes | olive oil |
| ¼ teaspoon freshly ground | Light Béchamel Sauce (page 78) |
| black pepper | Fresh Tomato Sauce (page 79) |
| 2 cups Basil, Fennel, and Garlic | ⅓ cup fresh basil, cut into strips |
| Chablis Blanc (page 18) | (optional) |

In a medium-size glass bowl, combine ricotta, egg, parsley, and pepper, mixing well. Cover and store in refrigerator until ready to use.

Reserve ½ cup of the wine. Pour ½ cup of the water and ½ cup of the wine into a large skillet. Bring to a simmer over low heat. Cook lasagne noodles 2 at a time in the skillet. When pliable, gently fold in half to ensure that the ends will be cooked. Cook 10 to 15 minutes, turning occasionally. Gently remove from skillet, drain, rinse, and drain again. Place on an oiled baking sheet until ready to assemble. Repeat with remaining noodles, adding equal parts water and wine as needed.

Preheat oven to 350°F. Place 2 noodles in an oiled casserole. Spread a quarter of the ricotta mixture over each noodle, then top with 2 more noodles. Place 2 additional noodles in another oiled casserole and spread with remaining ricotta mixture, then top with remaining noodles.

Pour ¼ cup of the reserved wine around edges of each casserole. Cover tightly with foil. Bake 20 minutes, or until cooked through.

To assemble, cut each lasagne strip into quarters or thirds. Spoon about 2 tablespoons of Light Béchamel Sauce onto individual plates. Place two pieces of lasagne bundles on sauce and top with a tablespoon of Fresh Tomato Sauce and basil, if desired.

# Polenta with Roasted Red Pepper Goat Cheese

*Serve as a main dish with a soup and green salad. Or cut into bite-size pieces and serve cold, warm, or heated through as an appetizer. If coarse-ground cornmeal isn't available, use all-purpose cornmeal — do not use fine-ground.*

▶ *Yield: 4 servings as an entrée, 6–8 as an appetizer*

> 3 tablespoons olive oil
> 2 cups Mixed Herbs and Garlic Chardonnay (page 14)
> 1 cup water
> 1 cup coarse-ground yellow cornmeal
> 3/4 cup grated Parmesan
> 1/2 teaspoon freshly ground black pepper
> 1 roasted red pepper, diced (page 50)
> 5 ounces goat cheese

Coat a 6-by-10-inch (or comparable size) ceramic baking dish with 1 table-spoon of the olive oil.

In a medium-size saucepan, bring wine and water to a boil over medium-high heat. Reduce heat to medium, and slowly stir in cornmeal. If cornmeal is very lumpy, mash with a potato masher. Cook, stirring constantly, about 10 minutes.

Remove from heat and stir in remaining 2 tablespoons of oil, grated Parmesan, and black pepper. Scrape into prepared baking dish and let cool completely.

Preheat oven to 350°F. In a small glass bowl, mix roasted red pepper and goat cheese until well blended. Cut polenta into bars or squares, and spread cheese mixture on top. Place on oiled baking sheet and bake until heated through, about 10 to 15 minutes. (Can be served without heating.)

# Roasted Red Pepper, Roasted Garlic, and Cheese Cornbread

*An unusual garlic-flavored cornbread, with the addition of provolone and Parmesan cheese. It can be easily reheated in the microwave: Wrap loosely with wax paper and heat at medium high about 2 minutes.*

▶ *Yield: serves 4–6*

- 1½ cups cornmeal
- ½ cup unbleached all-purpose flour
- 1 tablespoon baking powder
- 2 eggs
- ½ cup half-and-half
- ¾ cup Roasted Red Pepper and Garlic Chardonnay (page 12)
- 1 head (6–8 cloves) roasted garlic, mashed
- 1 roasted red pepper, diced (page 50)
- 1 cup shredded provolone
- ½ cup grated Parmesan

Grease an 8-inch square pan. Preheat oven to 425°F.

In a medium-size glass bowl, stir cornmeal, flour, and baking powder with a fork until well blended. In a separate bowl, beat eggs lightly. Add the half-and-half, wine, and roasted garlic. Stir the egg mixture into the cornmeal mixture until just moistened. Stir in roasted pepper, provolone, and Parmesan. Spread into prepared pan and bake 15 to 20 minutes.

# Herbal Cheese Rice Balls

*Give yourself time to prepare and cook these rice balls; it is worth the extra effort. They can be made a day or two ahead and reheated in a 300°F oven for 15 minutes.*

▶ *Yield: 8 rice balls*

| | |
|---|---|
| 1½ | cups Italian Herb Chardonnay (page 15) |
| ¾ | cup water |
| 1½ | cups instant long-grain rice |
| 1 | cup unbleached all-purpose flour |
| ¼ | pound mozzarella, cut into 8 half-inch cubes |
| 1 | large egg |
| ¼ | cup milk |
| | flavored bread crumbs (page 38) |
| | olive oil |

In a medium-size saucepan, bring wine and ½ cup of the water to a boil over high heat. Stir in rice. Remove from heat, cover, and let sit 5 minutes. Stir, cover, and let sit an additional 10 minutes. Transfer to a bowl, cover with plastic wrap, and chill.

Place rice in a large mixing bowl and blend in ¼ cup of the flour. With clean, floured hands, form a disk of rice in your palm. Position a cube of cheese in the center and cover with rice, gently but firmly forming a ball and completely enclosing the cheese. Set on a lightly floured platter. Repeat to form 8 balls. (You may have to wash and dry your hands several times during this process.) Chill rice balls for at least an hour.

In a glass pie plate or similar shallow rimmed plate, mix egg with milk and the remaining ¼ cup water.

Spread bread crumbs on a dinner plate. Gently coat rice balls in egg mixture, then cover in bread crumbs. If rice balls begin to fall apart, they can be molded back into shape once covered with crumbs.

Heat 1 inch of olive oil in a large saucepan. Over medium heat, fry 4 rice balls at a time until golden brown on all sides. Remove with a slotted spoon and drain on paper towels. Serve immediately or store in refrigerator until ready to reheat and serve.

# Herbal Wine Rice Pilaf

*The rosé tints the rice a delicate pink. If you prefer a more traditional appearance, use any of the white-wine mixtures. This dish can be made a day or two ahead and reheated in the microwave. Cook, covered, at medium about 5 to 8 minutes.*

▶ *Yield: 4–6 servings*

> 1 cup plus 2 tablespoons Chervil and Marjoram Rosé (page 28)
> 1/2 cup water
> 1 1/2 cups instant long-grain rice
> 3 tablespoons butter or margarine
> 1 small onion, chopped
> 2 stalks celery, diced
> 2 cups sliced mushrooms
> 2 tablespoons chopped fresh chervil (optional)

In a medium-size saucepan, bring 1 cup of the wine and water to a boil. Stir in rice, remove from heat, and cover. Let sit 5 minutes. Stir again and let cool.

In a large skillet over medium heat, mix the remaining 2 tablespoons of wine and 2 tablespoons of the butter until blended. Sauté onion and celery until tender, about 10 minutes. Reduce heat to low and add mushrooms. Cook, stirring occasionally, until mushrooms are tender, about 10 minutes. Add the remaining tablespoon of butter and rice. Stir thoroughly until heated through. If desired, add fresh chervil before serving.

# Three-Bean Chili

*As the flavors blend, this spicy chili will taste even better after a few days. For convenience, cook all dried beans together. The white beans will turn gray but will later turn pink when cooked in the tomato sauce. You can substitute canned beans for the dry, but the texture will not be the same.*

▶ *Yield: 6–8 servings*

| | |
|---|---|
| 8 | ounces dried black beans |
| 8 | ounces dried kidney beans |
| 8 | ounces dried white beans |
| 1 | onion, diced |
| 3 | tablespoons olive oil |
| 4 | cloves garlic, crushed |
| 1 | can (28 ounces) good-quality crushed tomatoes |
| 1 | can (4 ounces) diced green chilies |
| 2 | whole dried red chili peppers |
| 2 | cups Mixed Herb Burgundy (page 24) |
| 2 | dried red chili peppers, crushed |
| | grated cheddar or Monterey Jack cheese (optional) |

Pick over and rinse beans. Place beans in an 8-quart pot, and cover with 2 inches of water. Bring to a boil, and cook 5 minutes. Remove from heat, cover, and let sit 1½ hours. Drain, rinse, and drain again.

In an 8-quart pot over medium heat, sauté onion in olive oil about 10 minutes, or until tender. Add garlic and tomatoes and cook over medium heat until heated through. Add beans, green chilies, whole red chili peppers, and 1 cup of the wine. Bring to a simmer, reduce heat to low, cover, and cook, stirring occasionally, 45 minutes.

Stir in the remaining 1 cup of wine and crushed red chili peppers. Continue to simmer, stirring occasionally, 45 more minutes, or until chili has thickened. Remove whole chili peppers before serving. Top with shredded cheese to taste, if desired.

# Spicy Pinto Beans

*This spicy dish makes a tasty filling for tacos and is delicious served over rice.*
*The dried beans add texture, but you can substitute canned beans if you prefer.*
*Add some crushed dried chili peppers for extra "heat."*

▶ *Yield: 6–8 servings*

|   |   |
|---|---|
| 8 | ounces dried pinto beans |
| 3 | tablespoons olive oil |
| 2 | cups Chili Pepper and Garlic Pinot Noir (page 25) |
| 1 | onion, diced |
| 1 | sweet green pepper, diced |
| 3 | cloves garlic, sliced |
| 4 | chili peppers from wine mixture, diced |
| 2 | cups water |

Pick over beans and rinse. Place in a large pot, cover with 2 inches of water, and bring to a boil. Boil 5 minutes. Remove from heat, cover, and let sit 1 hour. Rinse well and drain.

Mix olive oil and ½ cup of the wine in a large skillet. Sauté onion, green pepper, garlic, and chili peppers over medium heat, about 10 minutes. Add beans and 2 cups of water. Cover and cook over low heat for 30 minutes, stirring occasionally. Add ¾ cup of the wine, cover, and cook an additional 30 minutes. Add remaining ¾ cup wine and cook, stirring often, 15 minutes until mixture has thickened.

# Herbed Rice and Cheese Soufflé

*The herbed rice gives this soufflé a delicate texture and additional flavor.*

▶ *Yield: 4 servings*

|   |   |
|---|---|
| 1 | cup Mixed Herb Chablis Blanc (page 17) |
| ¼ | cup water |
| 1 | cup instant long-grain rice |
| 2 | tablespoons butter or margarine |
| 3 | tablespoons unbleached all-purpose flour |
| ½ | cup half-and-half |
| 8 | ounces sharp cheddar cheese, shredded (2 cups) |
| 4 | eggs, separated |
|   | freshly ground black pepper |

In a small saucepan, bring ¾ cup of the wine and water to a boil. Add rice, cover, remove from heat, and let sit 5 minutes. Stir, let sit an additional 5 minutes. Set aside until ready to use.

Grease a 1½-quart soufflé dish. Preheat oven to 325°F.

In a medium-size saucepan, melt butter with the remaining ¼ cup wine over medium heat. With a wooden spoon, stir in flour to form a paste. Slowly add half-and-half, stirring constantly until mixture has thickened. Stir in cheese, continuing to stir until cheese melts. Remove from heat.

Beat egg yolks slightly in a small bowl. Stir into cheese mixture, then stir in rice. In a medium-size glass bowl, beat egg whites until soft peaks form. Fold into cheese-and-rice mixture. Pour into prepared soufflé dish. Bake 30 to 40 minutes until golden brown.

# Baked Custard Crepe Cups

*These crepes, made with wine, are placed in a muffin tin, filled with a flavorful custard, and then baked in the oven. They can be made ahead and easily reheated in a 300°F oven for 20 minutes. They make a wonderful presentation.*

▶ *Yield: 16 crepe cups*

### Crepes
|   |   |
|---|---|
| 6 | eggs |
| 1⅓ | cups unbleached all-purpose flour |
| 1 | cup milk |
| 1 | cup Rosemary Chablis Blanc (page 17) |

### Custard Filling
|   |   |
|---|---|
| 8 | ounces mushrooms, sliced |
| ¾ | cup Rosemary Chablis Blanc |
| 8 | ounces ham, diced |
| 2 | packages (each 10 ounces) frozen chopped spinach, defrosted and drained |
| 6 | large eggs |
| 1 | cup sour cream |
| 1 | cup mayonnaise |
| 8 | ounces cheddar or Monterey Jack cheese, shredded (2 cups) |

**To make crepes:** Beat eggs slightly in a medium-size glass bowl. Stir in flour, milk, and 1 cup wine. Let stand 30 minutes.

Pour scant ¼ cup of crepe batter into a lightly greased 8-inch skillet. Cook over low heat until top of crepe is dry and bottom is slightly brown. Turn onto plate. Repeat process using all of batter. As crepes cool, stack between layers of wax paper.

**To make custard filling:** In a large skillet over medium heat, sauté mushrooms in ¼ cup of the wine for about 10 minutes. Reduce heat to low, add ham and spinach. Cook until all liquid is reduced and mixture is heated through. Remove from heat and cool slightly.

Beat the eggs in a medium-size glass bowl. Stir in remaining ½ cup wine, sour cream, and mayonnaise; beat until smooth. Add spinach mixture and cheese, blending well.

Grease muffin tin. Preheat oven to 350°F. To assemble crepe cups, place each crepe in a prepared muffin cup, gently shaping to fit. Fill three-quarters full with custard mixture. Bake 30 to 40 minutes until custard is set. Cool slightly before removing each crepe cup from muffin tin.

# Onion and Zucchini Tart

*This delectable tart is filled with onions and zucchini flavored by sautéing in a wine mixture. The tart can be made ahead and reheated, covered with foil, in a 300°F oven for 20 minutes.*

▶ *Yield: 6–8 servings*

>      pastry for a 10-inch pie crust
> 3   large onions, sliced
> 1   pound zucchini, peeled and sliced
> 1   cup Rosemary and Garlic Chardonnay (page 14)
> 4   large eggs
> 8   ounces sour cream
> 8   ounces provolone, sliced
>      freshly ground black pepper

Preheat oven to 250°F. Roll out pie crust to fit a tart pan with removable bottom. Bake about 15 minutes, or until set. Cool. Increase oven temperature to 350°F.

In a large skillet over medium heat, sauté onions and zucchini in ½ cup of the wine until they are tender and the liquid has evaporated, about 20 minutes. Spread on bottom of pie crust.

In a medium-size glass bowl, mix eggs with remaining ½ cup wine. Add sour cream and blend well. Top onion-zucchini mixture with slices of provolone. Gently pour egg mixture over cheese and sprinkle with pepper to taste.

Bake 1 hour, or until filling is firm and golden brown.

# Broccoli and Monterey Jack Quiche

*Wine and mayonnaise give this quiche a very light texture. You can substitute low-fat dairy products for a less fattening version.*

▶ *Yield: 6–8 servings*

|   | |
|---|---|
|   | pastry for a 10-inch pie crust |
| 1 | cup sour cream |
| ½ | cup mayonnaise |
| ½ | cup Lemon Dill Rhine Wine (page 19) |
| 3 | large eggs |
| 1 | pound broccoli florets, cooked and chopped |
| 8 | ounces Monterey Jack cheese, shredded (2 cups) |

Preheat oven to 250°F. Roll out pie crust to fit quiche pan with removable bottom. Bake 10 to 15 minutes, or until set. Cool slightly. Increase oven temperature to 350°F.

Mix sour cream and mayonnaise with a wire whisk. Stir in wine. Add eggs, one at a time, beating well after each addition.

Spread broccoli evenly on pie crust and sprinkle with cheese. Gently pour egg mixture over cheese and broccoli. Bake 1 hour, or until filling is firm to the touch. Cool on rack about 20 minutes. Remove from quiche pan.

# Chapter Ten

# Vegetables

*My vegetable love should grow vaster than empires,*
*and more slow.*

— Andrew Marvell

Vegetables are a mainstay in cooking, from raw to roasted, with sautéed, stewed, mashed, pureed, broiled, and grilled in between. Of course, there's no comparison to fresh vegetables, but frozen vegetables do serve a purpose. Peeling, coring, and seeding are eliminated, which saves time. Many of the name-brand frozen vegetables may be used in some recipes; however, it's best not to substitute frozen vegetables for the fresh vegetables in these recipes.

With a few exceptions, the recipes in this chapter call for fresh vegetables. In these recipes, it does make a difference. 🍇

# Herb and Garlic Mashed Potatoes

*Basic mashed potatoes, only this time the potatoes are cooked in a flavored wine mixture. Use low-fat margarine and substitute 1 cup of fat-free sour cream for a lighter version.*

▶ *Yield: 4 servings*

|     |                                          |
| --- | ---------------------------------------- |
| 2   | pounds white potatoes                    |
| 1½  | cups Italian Herb Chardonnay (page 15)   |
| 4–6 | cloves garlic, crushed                   |
| 4   | tablespoons butter or margarine          |
| ½   | teaspoon freshly ground black pepper     |

Peel, wash, and quarter potatoes. Place in a medium-size glass or ceramic baking dish. Pour 1 cup of the wine over, and cover tightly with plastic wrap. Cook 20 minutes at medium heat in the microwave, turning and stirring potatoes every 5 minutes.

Place potatoes and cooking liquid in a medium-size glass bowl. Add garlic and mash. Add butter, the remaining ½ cup wine, and pepper. Stir until well blended.

# Herb-Baked Potatoes au Gratin

*A good dish to bake ahead, the gratin can be covered with foil and reheated in a 300°F oven for 20 minutes. For a delicious alternative to hash browns, reheat in a skillet over medium heat with 2 tablespoons of butter or oil.*

▶ *Yield: 4–6 servings*

|     |                                          |
| --- | ---------------------------------------- |
| 2   | pounds white baking potatoes, peeled, rinsed, and sliced thin |
| 1   | cup Rosemary Chablis Blanc (page 17)     |
| ¾   | cup water                                |
| 1   | tablespoon olive oil                     |
| ⅓   | cup chopped scallions                    |
| 1   | cup grated Swiss, cheddar, or Monterey Jack cheese (or any combination) freshly ground black pepper |
| ½   | cup flavored bread crumbs (page 38)      |

Place potatoes in a medium-size saucepan with ¾ cup of the wine and water. Bring to a boil and cook for 5 minutes. Drain, reserving ¾ cup liquid. Rinse potatoes.

Coat a medium-size baking dish with olive oil. Place half of the potatoes in an overlapping layer in the dish. Sprinkle with half of the scallions, half of the cheese, and pepper to taste. Repeat layers.

Preheat oven to 350°F. Add the remaining ¼ cup wine to ¾ cup reserved liquid, and gently pour evenly over potatoes. Cover with foil and bake 1 hour. Remove foil and increase oven temperature to 400°F. Sprinkle with bread crumbs, and bake 10 minutes, or until golden brown.

# Ratatouille

*This dish can be served hot, warm, or cold. Serve as an appetizer, a topping for beef, chicken, pork, or fish, in sandwiches, on pizza, or as a side dish. Ratatouille is an excellent make-ahead dish, and can be reheated in the microwave: Just place in a glass casserole, cover with wax paper, and cook at medium about 10 minutes, stirring several times.*

▶ *Yield: 6–8 servings*

| | |
|---|---|
| 2 | tablespoons olive oil |
| 1½ | cups Mixed Herbs and Garlic Merlot (page 24) |
| 3 | onions, sliced |
| 2 | sweet green peppers, cored, seeded, and cut into 1-inch strips |
| 6 | cloves garlic, sliced |
| 1 | pound zucchini, peeled and sliced |
| 1 | pound eggplant, peeled and cut into 1-inch cubes |
| 3 | large tomatoes, peeled and chopped |

In a large skillet over medium heat, blend olive oil and ½ cup of the wine. Add onions, green peppers, and garlic, and cook, stirring occasionally, about 15 minutes. Reduce heat to low and stir in zucchini, eggplant, and an additional ½ cup of the wine. Cook, covered, for 30 minutes, stirring occasionally.

Increase heat to medium. Add tomatoes and the remaining ½ cup wine. Cook, stirring often, until liquid is reduced and ratatouille has slightly thickened.

# Vegetable Pot Pie

*This pie can be made with an assortment of vegetables, as long as the quantities are consistent with those in the recipe.*

▶ *Yield: 4–6 servings*

|        | pastry for two 10-inch pie crusts |
|--------|-----------------------------------|
| 1½     | cups Mixed Herbs and Garlic Rosé (page 29) |
| 3      | carrots, peeled and sliced thin   |
| 3      | tablespoons olive oil             |
| 1      | large onion, sliced and quartered |
| 2      | medium zucchini, peeled and sliced thin |
| 1      | cup sliced mushrooms              |
| 3      | cloves garlic, sliced             |
| 1      | tablespoon butter or margarine    |
| 1      | tablespoon unbleached all-purpose flour |
| 6      | ounces sharp cheddar cheese, sliced |
|        | freshly ground black pepper       |

## Variations

For a variety of flavors, don't hesitate to try different ingredients. Substitute Monterey Jack cheese for the cheddar, and replace the carrots and zucchini with 2 large red peppers and 1 large green pepper, cored, seeded, and sliced lengthwise. For a more distinctive flavor, try blue cheese, omit the carrots, and add an additional large onion. Or use goat cheese, omit carrots and zucchini, and add 2 large red peppers, cored, seeded, and sliced lengthwise.

In a small covered glass or ceramic casserole, cook carrots with ¼ cup of the wine for 6 minutes at medium-high in microwave, stirring once.

In a large skillet over medium heat, combine olive oil and ½ cup of the wine. Add onion, zucchini, carrots (and cooking liquid), mushrooms, and garlic. Cover and cook, stirring occasionally, until vegetables are tender, about 20 minutes. Let cool.

Preheat oven to 350°F. Line bottom of pie pan with pastry crust. Transfer vegetables with a slotted spoon to bottom crust of pie pan. Add the remaining ¾ cup wine to reserved liquid in skillet, and cook over low heat, stirring in butter and flour. Cook, stirring constantly, until slightly thickened and reduced to about ½ cup. Pour over vegetables. Top with cheese and pepper to taste. Cover with second pie crust, sealing edges well. With a sharp knife, cut several slits in top to vent. Bake about 45 minutes, or until crust is golden brown.

# Vegetable-Stuffed Eggplant

*For individual servings as a main dish, use 2 smaller eggplants cut in half, and serve with a leafy salad and crusty bread.*

▶ *Yield: 4–6 servings*

| | |
|---|---|
| 1 | large eggplant (about 1½ pounds) |
| 4 | tablespoons olive oil |
| 4 | cloves garlic, sliced |
| 1 | cup Thyme, Tarragon, and Chive Cabernet Sauvignon (page 26) |
| ½ | onion, chopped |
| 1 | large tomato, diced |
| ½ | cup flavored bread crumbs (page 38) |
| | grated Parmesan |

Preheat oven to 350°F. Peel eggplant and slice in half lengthwise. Brush each half with 1 tablespoon of the olive oil, place in a baking pan, cut side up, and top with 2 cloves of the sliced garlic. Wrap tightly with foil. Bake 30 minutes. Let cool. Scoop out center of each half and dice. Coat a large baking dish with 1 tablespoon of the oil. Set eggplant shells in dish.

Blend remaining 2 tablespoons of oil and ½ cup of the wine in a large skillet over medium heat. Add onion, remaining garlic, tomato, and diced eggplant. Sauté about 15 minutes, until vegetables are tender. Remove from heat. Stir in bread crumbs and remaining ½ cup of wine. Divide filling between eggplant shells. Sprinkle with grated cheese to taste.

Bake 10 to 15 minutes until heated through. Let cool slightly. Cut into 3-inch-wide slices.

# Roasted Vegetable Sandwich with Dipping Sauce

*The pan that the vegetables are roasted in is deglazed with an herbal wine to create an incredible sauce. The recipe calls for crusty rolls, but you can use a loaf of bread. Slice bread horizontally, fill with vegetables, sprinkle with grated cheese, and cover with top of bread.*

▶ *Yield: 4 servings*

| | |
|---|---|
| ½ | cup olive oil |
| 1 | large zucchini, peeled and sliced lengthwise |
| 1 | small eggplant, peeled and sliced lengthwise |
| 1 | red onion, quartered |
| 2 | large tomatoes, quartered |
| 1½ | cups Sage and Garlic Rosé (page 28) |
| 3 | cloves garlic, sliced |
| | grated Parmesan |
| 4 | large crusty rolls, split |

Preheat broiler. Coat 11-by-14-inch rimmed baking pan with 2 tablespoons of the olive oil. Place zucchini, eggplant, onion, and tomatoes in pan, and drizzle with remaining oil. Roast under broiler, turning until both sides are browned. Watch carefully, and remove vegetables to platter as they brown. The tomatoes and onions will take the longest to roast.

When vegetables are cooked, place empty pan with drippings on stovetop over medium heat. Slowly pour wine into pan, stirring with vegetable bits remaining in pan. Add garlic and cook until liquid is a rich brown and has incorporated all vegetable drippings.

Divide vegetables among split rolls. Sprinkle with cheese to taste, and cover with top of roll. Pour sauce into small individual serving bowls. Serve sandwich with dipping sauce.

# Steamed Broccoli

*This easy recipe is also the first step in making Breaded Broccoli, below.*

▶ *Yield: 4 servings*

1   pound broccoli florets, rinsed and drained
½   cup Parsley, Chive, and Lemon Rhine Wine (page 20)

Place broccoli in a medium-size glass or ceramic baking dish. Pour wine over and cover with wax paper. Cook at medium-high in microwave for 3 minutes, stirring once. Drain and serve.


# Breaded Broccoli

*This flavored, steamed broccoli, coated with bread crumbs and fried with garlic in olive oil, can be made ahead and reheated in a 300°F oven for 10 to 15 minutes. It also tastes great cold.*

▶ *Yield: 4–6 servings*

1   pound broccoli florets, rinsed and drained
¾   cup Parsley, Chive, and Lemon Rhine Wine (page 20)
1   large egg
¼   cup grated Parmesan
½   cup unbleached all-purpose flour
1   cup flavored bread crumbs (page 38)
   olive oil
3   cloves garlic, sliced

Prepare recipe for Steamed Broccoli, above, using ½ cup of the wine. Let cool. Strain, reserving liquid.

In a glass pie plate, mix egg, reserved liquid, remaining ¼ cup wine, and grated cheese until well blended. Lightly coat broccoli florets in flour, roll in egg mixture, and cover with bread crumbs.

Pour ½ inch of olive oil into a large skillet and add a few slices of garlic. Add broccoli and fry over medium heat, turning to brown both sides. Add oil and more garlic, as required. Drain broccoli on paper towels.

# Caramelized Onions

*Use in sandwiches, fajitas, and salads, or as a topping for potatoes, beef, pork, chicken, or pizza.*

▶ *Yield: about 1½ cups*

> 1¼ cups Rosemary and Black Peppercorn Rosé (page 30)
> 3 large onions, sliced ¼ inch thick

Pour ¼ cup of the wine into a large skillet. Separate rings of onion slices, and place in skillet. Cook over low heat, covered, for 10 to 15 minutes, stirring occasionally. Add another ½ cup of the wine and continue to cook an additional 10 minutes.

Raise heat to high, add the remaining ½ cup wine, and cook, stirring constantly, until onions are golden brown and liquid has evaporated.

# Caramelized Carrots

*This side dish can be prepared ahead and reheated in the microwave. Cover with wax paper, and cook at medium about 6 minutes, stirring once.*

▶ *Yield: 4 servings*

> 2 tablespoons butter or margarine
> 1 cup Parsley and Savory Rosé (page 29)
> 1 pound carrots, peeled and sliced thin

Melt butter with ½ cup of the wine in a large skillet over medium heat. Add carrots, increase heat to high, and cook, stirring often, until liquid has evaporated. Add the remaining ½ cup wine, and cook, stirring constantly, until carrots are golden brown and liquid has evaporated.

# Stuffed Vidalia Onions

*Vidalia onions add a sweetness to this dish.*

▶ *Yield: 4 servings*

        4    medium Vidalia onions
        1    cup Oregano, Fennel, and Garlic Chardonnay (page 15)
        1    cup flavored bread crumbs (page 38)
       ½    cup chopped mushrooms
       ½    cup grated Parmesan

Remove peel from onions. Trim about ¼ inch from root end, keeping whole onion intact. Place in a small glass or ceramic baking dish. Pour ½ cup of the wine over onions and cover with wax paper. Cook at medium-high in microwave for 10 minutes, or until fork-tender, turning dish once during cooking process. Transfer to platter to cool. Reserve cooking liquid.

Cut ½ inch from top of onion and scoop out center, leaving at least two layers of outer rings. Return "shells" to baking dish. Chop centers of onions.

Preheat oven to 350°F. In a medium-size bowl, mix bread crumbs with reserved cooking liquid to moisten. Stir in chopped onion, mushrooms, and cheese. Fill onion shells with mixture.

Pour the remaining ½ cup wine over onions, cover with foil, and bake 30 minutes.

Vidalia onions are sweet onions grown in Georgia. If they are unavailable, substitute Walla Walla, Maui, Texas Sweets, or any other type of sweet onion.

# Spinach and Roasted Garlic Timbales

*An elegant side dish that can be prepared up to a day ahead. For an appetizer, spoon the spinach-garlic mixture into greased mini muffin tins. These freeze well, wrapped tightly in foil, for up to 2 weeks. When ready to serve, defrost before reheating in a 300°F oven for 20 minutes. Substitute low-fat cream cheese and fat-free sour cream for a lighter version.*

▶ *Yield: 12 timbales*

|     |                                                      |
|-----|------------------------------------------------------|
| 1   | package (10 ounces) frozen chopped spinach           |
| 8   | ounces cream cheese, softened                        |
| 8   | ounces sour cream                                    |
| 6–8 | cloves roasted garlic                                |
| 3   | eggs                                                 |
| ½   | cup Parsley and Sage Chardonnay (page 14)            |
| ¼   | teaspoon freshly ground black pepper                 |
| ¼   | cup finely chopped fresh parsley (optional)          |

Cook spinach according to package directions. Cool and drain well.

In a medium-size glass bowl, blend cream cheese, sour cream, and roasted garlic. In a small bowl, thoroughly mix eggs and wine. Add to garlic mixture. Stir in spinach and pepper.

Preheat oven to 375°F. Generously grease muffin tin. Spoon spinach mixture into muffin cups, three-quarters full. Bake 20 minutes, or until timbales are firm in center. Let cool 5 minutes. Loosen edges and invert on a baking sheet. Transfer to serving platter and sprinkle with parsley, if desired.

# Marinated Smoked Mushrooms

*A quick, easy side dish that can be made ahead and served cold, warm, or hot with steak or chicken. Have plenty of crusty bread available to soak up the sauce.*

▶ *Yield: about 1 cup*

| | |
|---|---|
| 1 | tablespoon butter or margarine |
| ½ | cup Basil, Fennel, and Garlic Chablis Blanc (page 18) |
| 8 | ounces mushrooms, rinsed, dried, and sliced |
| | liquid smoke |
| | freshly ground black pepper |
| 1 | tablespoon chopped fresh basil (optional) |

In a small saucepan, melt butter with wine over medium heat. Add mushrooms and cook, stirring often, about 10 minutes, or until mushrooms are tender. Remove from heat. Stir in liquid-smoke flavoring to taste, a few drops at a time. Sprinkle with pepper and fresh basil, if desired.

# Green Beans and Bread Crumbs

*This flavorful side dish can be paired with beef, chicken, pork, or fish.*

▶ *Yield: 4–6 servings*

| | |
|---|---|
| 2 | tablespoons olive oil |
| ½ | cup Mixed Herbs and Garlic Rosé (page 29) |
| 3 | cloves garlic, sliced |
| 1 | pound good-quality canned french-cut green beans, drained |
| ¾ | cup flavored bread crumbs (page 38) |
| | freshly ground black pepper |

Combine olive oil and wine in a medium-size skillet. Add garlic and cook until tender, about 10 minutes. Add green beans; cook until heated through. Stir in bread crumbs until moistened. Sprinkle with pepper to taste.

# Creamy Cauliflower Casserole

*A creamy mixture of cauliflower and cheddar and Parmesan cheese. Use either fresh or frozen cauliflower.*

▶ *Yield: 4 servings*

|     |                                      |
| --- | ------------------------------------ |
| 1   | pound cauliflower florets            |
| 1/2 | cup Parsley and Sage Chardonnay (page 14) |
| 1   | cup sour cream                       |
| 1/2 | cup shredded cheddar cheese          |
| 1/3 | cup grated Parmesan                  |
| 1/4 | cup chopped scallions                |
|     | freshly ground black or white pepper |

Place cauliflower in a medium-size casserole. Pour wine over, cover with wax paper, and microwave at medium-high 6 to 8 minutes, or until tender, turning once. Drain and reserve liquid; set cauliflower aside.

Butter a medium-size casserole. Preheat oven to 400°F.

In a medium-size glass bowl, combine sour cream with reserved cooking liquid. Add cheddar and Parmesan, scallions, and pepper to taste. Mix in cauliflower. Pour into prepared casserole. Bake 30 minutes, or until golden brown and bubbly.

# Brussels Sprouts, Bacon, and Cheese Puff

*Guaranteed to convert just about anyone into a lover of Brussels sprouts.*

▶ *Yield: 2–4 servings*

    1    package (10 ounces) frozen Brussels sprouts
    ½   cup Basil Chardonnay (page 12)
    ¼   cup crumbled cooked bacon
    ½   cup shredded Swiss cheese
    2    eggs
    ¼   cup mayonnaise
         freshly ground black pepper

Preheat oven to 300°F.

Place frozen Brussels sprouts in a small casserole dish. Pour ¼ cup of the wine over, cover with wax paper, and cook at medium-high in the microwave about 6 minutes, turning once. Drain, coarsely chop, and return to clean casserole dish. Top with bacon and Swiss cheese.

Lightly mix eggs in a small bowl. Add mayonnaise, remaining ¼ cup wine, and pepper, mixing until well blended. Pour evenly over Brussels sprouts mixture. Bake 20 minutes, or until golden brown and puffed.

## Fresh or Frozen?

Frozen Brussels sprouts are very tender and reduce the cooking time in the first step of preparation. Fresh Brussels sprouts may be used as long as they are cooked until tender before being chopped.

# Chapter Eleven

# Chicken, Beef, and Pork

*You'll have no scandal while you dine,*
*But honest talk and wholesome wine.*

— Lord Tennyson

Whether used in a marinade, as a cooking liquid, or as an ingredient in a sauce, flavored wine imparts its distinctive taste to chicken, beef, or pork.

The recipes in this chapter offer a variety of methods for using the flavored wines. In most of the recipes, the meat or poultry is marinated in the wine mixture, while in others the flavored wine is used for sauces.

Either way, the flavored wine will subtly infuse its seasonings into the meat or poultry.

# Chicken Fajitas with Roasted Red and Yellow Peppers

*Make the roasted peppers a day or two ahead. If you marinate the chicken early in the day, this dish can be prepared in less than 30 minutes.*

▶ *Yield: 6 fajitas*

| | |
|---|---|
| 1 | cup Cilantro, Lime, and Garlic Rhine Wine (page 19) |
| 3 | tablespoons olive oil |
| 1 | pound chicken tenders |
| 1 | large onion, sliced |
| 4 | cloves garlic, sliced |
| 6 | flour tortillas |
| 4 | ounces Monterey Jack cheese, shredded (1 cup) |
| 2 | roasted red peppers, sliced lengthwise (page 50) |
| 2 | roasted yellow peppers, sliced lengthwise (page 50) |

In a small bowl, mix ½ cup of the wine and 1 tablespoon of the olive oil with a fork. Place chicken tenders in a small glass or ceramic casserole. Pour wine mixture over chicken. Cover with plastic wrap, and let marinate in refrigerator at least 2 hours, turning once.

Bring chicken to room temperature. In a large skillet, combine remaining 2 tablespoons of oil and ¼ cup of the wine. Add onion and cook, stirring occasionally, until tender, about 10 minutes. Push onion to one side of pan and add chicken. Increase heat to high, and quickly brown chicken on both sides. Add garlic and the remaining ¼ cup of wine. Stir well and cook mixture over medium heat until liquid is slightly reduced and thickened.

To assemble, heat tortillas in microwave according to package directions. Spoon chicken mixture down center of each tortilla, sprinkle with cheese, and top with some red and yellow roasted peppers. Fold edges over filling.

## Freezing Chicken Breasts

To save time, chicken breasts can be trimmed ahead of time and frozen, then defrosted just before preparing the recipe. Many supermarkets now offer individually frozen chicken breasts.

# Chicken Rosé with Parsley and Garlic Focaccia

*Another great do-ahead dish: Keep wrapped tightly in foil for up to 2 hours before serving. The focaccia recipe will make two focacce. Reserve one for later use: Wrap tightly in a double layer of foil, freeze, and use within 2 weeks.*

▶ *Yield: 4 servings*

### Focaccia

| | |
|---|---|
| 3/4 | cup Parsley and Garlic Rosé (page 28) |
| 1/4 | cup hot water |
| 1 | package active dry yeast |
| 2 | tablespoons parsley flakes |
| 2½–3 | cups unbleached all-purpose flour |
| 2 | tablespoons olive oil |

In a large mixing bowl, combine wine, water, and yeast. Let yeast proof 15 to 20 minutes, or until completely dissolved. Add parsley flakes, and mix in flour until a soft dough forms. Knead 5 minutes with a dough hook, or 15 minutes by hand. Dough will be slightly sticky and elastic.

Pour 1 tablespoon olive oil into a large glass bowl. Place dough in bowl, turning to coat. Cover with wax paper, set in a warm place, and let rise until doubled in bulk, about 1½ hours.

Punch dough down, divide in half, placing each half in an oiled 9-inch round cake pan. Spread dough to edges of pan. Brush dough with oil, cover with wax paper, set in a warm place, and let rise 1 hour. Bake in a preheated 400°F oven for about 20 minutes, or until light golden brown.

### Chicken Rosé

| | |
|---|---|
| 1 | cup Parsley and Garlic Rosé (page 28) |
| 4 | tablespoons olive oil |
| 1 | pound skinless, boneless chicken breasts, pounded thin |
| 1 | medium onion, sliced |
| 8 | ounces mushrooms, rinsed and sliced |
| 6 | ounces provolone, sliced |

Mix ½ cup of the wine and 2 tablespoons of the olive oil with a fork until blended. Place chicken in a medium-size glass baking dish. Pour marinade over and cover with plastic wrap. Let marinate in refrigerator at least 2 hours. Bring to room temperature before cooking.

In a large skillet over medium heat, blend the remaining 2 tablespoons olive oil and ¼ cup of the wine. Add onion and mushrooms and cook, covered, for about 15 minutes, or until tender. Remove onion-mushroom mixture from skillet and place chicken breasts in skillet. Cook over medium-high heat about 10 minutes, browning on both sides. Add onion-mushroom mixture and the remaining ¼ cup wine. Cook, stirring often, until liquid is reduced, about 10 minutes.

To assemble, slice focaccia in half horizontally. Place chicken breasts on bottom, spread with onion-mushroom mixture, layer cheese over, and cover with top of focaccia. Serve immediately, or wrap tightly in foil to serve within several hours.

# Chicken Merlot with Caramelized Onions

*The seasoned richness of the Merlot is absorbed by the chicken and onions.*

▶ *Yield: 4 servings*

| | |
|---|---|
| 4 | tablespoons butter or margarine |
| 1¼ | cups Mixed Herbs and Garlic Merlot (page 24) |
| 3 | medium onions, sliced |
| 1 | pound skinless, boneless chicken breasts, pounded thin |

In a large skillet over medium heat, melt 2 tablespoons of the butter with ¼ cup of the wine. Add onions, cover, and cook, stirring occasionally, until tender, about 15 minutes. Increase heat to high, add an additional ½ cup of the wine, and cook, stirring often, until onions turn golden brown and liquid has evaporated. Transfer to platter.

Reduce heat to medium, melt the remaining 2 tablespoons of butter, and add chicken. Sauté, turning once, until cooked through and rosy brown. Remove to platter, placing on top of onions. Slowly pour the remaining ½ cup of wine into skillet with drippings, and deglaze pan, stirring to loosen bits of chicken until sauce thickens. Pour sauce over chicken and onions. Serve immediately.

# Chicken Pot Pie in Pastry Crust

*The wine in the pastry produces a delicate, flaky crust. The chicken filling is delectable.*

▶ *Yield: 4–6 servings*

### Pastry Crust

2½ cups unbleached all-purpose flour
1 cup shortening
7–8 tablespoons Mixed Herb Chablis Blanc (page 17)

### Chicken Filling

1 pound skinless, boneless chicken breasts
1⅔ cups Mixed Herb Chablis Blanc
2 carrots, peeled and sliced thin
1 small onion, chopped
1 cup sliced mushrooms
1 cup fresh, frozen, or canned peas
2 tablespoons butter or margarine
¼ cup unbleached all-purpose flour
½ cup half-and-half

**To make pastry:** Place flour in a large glass bowl and cut in shortening. Add wine, 1 tablespoon at a time, until dough holds together. Wrap in wax paper and refrigerate for at least 1 hour.

**To make chicken filling:** In a large covered skillet over medium heat, cook chicken breasts in ½ cup of the wine for about 10 minutes, turning once. Transfer to platter and let cool. Cut into bite-size pieces.

Add an additional ½ cup of the wine to skillet, and sauté carrots, covered, stirring occasionally, about 10 minutes, or until slightly tender. Add onion and mushrooms. Simmer, covered, over low heat, until tender, about 10 minutes. Add peas and chicken. Cover and remove from heat.

In a small saucepan over low heat, melt butter. Add flour to make a roux, and slowly stir in the remaining ⅔ cup of wine. Stir in half-and-half. Continue to stir until slightly thickened. Mix into chicken-vegetable mixture.

Preheat oven to 350°F. Divide dough in half. Pat or roll out each half of dough into a circle to fit a 9-inch pie plate. Line pie plate with one circle of dough. Fill with chicken-vegetable mixture. Top with second circle of dough. Seal edges tightly. With a sharp knife, cut several slits in top crust to vent. Bake 30 to 45 minutes, until golden brown. Let cool about 5 minutes before cutting.

# Oven-Baked Breaded Chicken with Roasted Red Pepper Mayonnaise

*The flavored mayonnaise, also excellent as a sandwich spread, can be made several days before serving. The chicken can be baked earlier in the day and reheated in a 300°F oven for about 10 minutes.*

▶ *Yield: 4 servings*

### Oven-Baked Breaded Chicken
- 1 cup Roasted Red Pepper and Garlic Chardonnay (page 12)
- 2 tablespoons olive oil
- 1 pound skinless, boneless chicken breasts, pounded thin
- 1 large egg
- 1 cup bread crumbs
  olive oil for baking

Blend ½ cup of the wine with olive oil. Place chicken in a large glass or ceramic baking dish. Pour wine marinade over, cover with plastic wrap, and refrigerate for at least 4 hours, turning several times. Remove from refrigerator 20 minutes before preparing.

In a pie plate, mix egg with the remaining ½ cup of wine until well blended. Place bread crumbs on a platter. Coat chicken breasts with egg mixture, then cover in bread crumbs, coating well.

Preheat oven to 300°F. Coat rimmed baking sheet with a thin layer of oil, and heat in oven until oil is hot. Place chicken breasts on baking sheet, and bake, turning once, until both sides are browned, about 20 minutes. Serve with Roasted Red Pepper Mayonnaise, below.

### Roasted Red Pepper Mayonnaise
- ½ roasted red pepper (page 50)
- 1 cup mayonnaise
- 1 teaspoon dried basil

Puree red pepper in mini chopper. Place mayonnaise in a small glass bowl. Stir in red pepper and basil, mixing thoroughly until well blended. Refrigerate until ready to serve.

# Baked Chicken Sandwich

*This can be made earlier in the day and travels well to picnics. Just wrap sandwich tightly with a double layer of foil.*

▶ *Yield: 4 servings*

- 2 pounds skinless, boneless chicken breasts
- 3/4 cup Sun-Dried Tomato and Garlic Merlot (page 25)
- 1 tablespoon olive oil
- 1 baguette (10 ounces)
- 3 ounces goat cheese
- red leaf lettuce

Pound chicken breasts thin, and place in a single layer in a baking dish. In a small bowl, mix ½ cup of the wine and olive oil with a fork until well blended. Pour over chicken. Cover with plastic wrap and refrigerate. Allow to marinate at least 2 hours, turning chicken once. Remove from refrigerator 20 minutes before preparing.

Preheat broiler. Place chicken on a rimmed baking sheet. Baste with one-third of marinade. Broil until browned, about 6 minutes. Turn chicken, spoon the remaining marinade over, and return to broiler for an additional 5 minutes, or until cooked through. Remove chicken to platter.

Deglaze baking sheet with the remaining ¼ cup wine, cooking until liquid is reduced by half. Pour sauce evenly over chicken. Let sit at least 10 minutes.

Split baguette and spread goat cheese on both halves. Top bottom half with chicken and lettuce; cover with top of baguette. Cut into four pieces.

# Sautéed Chicken with Herbal Wine Sauce

*The wine sauce delicately flavors the chicken. Experiment with various wine mixtures, such as Orange Mango Chardonnay, or Herb, Lemon, and Garlic Chablis Blanc, or any of the other flavored mixtures for an unusual, tasty dish.*

▶ *Yield: 4 servings*

| | |
|---|---|
| 1 | pound skinless, boneless chicken breasts, pounded thin |
| 1/2 | cup unbleached all-purpose flour |
| 2 | tablespoons butter or margarine |
| 3 | tablespoons olive oil |
| 3/4 | cup Parsley and Sage Chardonnay (page 14) |
| | freshly ground black pepper |
| 1/4 | cup chopped fresh parsley (optional) |

Coat both sides of chicken with flour. In a large skillet over medium heat, melt butter with olive oil. Sauté chicken until golden brown on both sides, about 15 minutes. Transfer to serving plate.

Add wine to skillet. Cook over low heat, deglazing pan. Stir well until liquid is slightly thick. Add chicken and cook several minutes on each side. Transfer chicken to serving plate, and spoon sauce over chicken. Sprinkle with pepper to taste and fresh parsley, if desired.

Flattening chicken breasts is easy with this method. Lay two chicken breasts in a 1-gallon food-storage bag. Pound with a mallet to desired thickness, remove, and repeat with additional chicken breasts. If you don't have a mallet, use the side of a sturdy mug or a saucepan.

# Chicken-Stuffed Red Pepper Halves

*Although green peppers may be substituted for the red peppers, the taste and presentation of the dish will change. The recipe for the chicken stuffing makes more than needed to fill the peppers. Leftover stuffing can be formed into patties and fried in butter or margarine until browned on both sides.*

▶ *Yield: 6–8 servings*

|       |                                        |
|-------|----------------------------------------|
| 2     | pounds skinless, boneless chicken breasts |
| 1⅓    | cups Italian Herb Chardonnay (page 15) |
| 1     | tablespoon olive oil                   |
| 1     | tablespoon butter or margarine         |
| ¾     | cup diced onion                        |
| 4     | sweet red peppers                      |
| 8     | ounces cream cheese, softened          |
| 2     | eggs, slightly beaten                  |
| ½     | cup chopped scallions                  |
| 1     | cup bread crumbs                       |
|       | freshly ground black pepper            |
|       | olive oil                              |

Place chicken in a single layer in a large baking dish. In a small bowl, mix ⅔ cup of the wine and 1 tablespoon olive oil with a fork until well blended. Pour marinade over chicken, cover with plastic wrap, and refrigerate. Allow to marinate at least 6 hours or overnight, turning once.

In a medium-size skillet, melt butter with ⅓ cup wine over medium heat. Add onion, and cook, stirring occasionally, until tender, about 10 minutes. Set aside.

Cut peppers in half lengthwise. Remove core, seeds, and excess membrane. Rinse and pat dry. Set aside.

Cut chicken into quarters and chop in a food processor with a pulse motion. (Do not grind fine.) Transfer chicken to a large glass bowl. Add onion, cream cheese, eggs, scallions, bread crumbs, the remaining ⅓ cup of wine, and black pepper, mixing thoroughly with a fork after each addition.

Preheat oven to 375°F. Stuff pepper halves with chicken mixture. Place stuffed peppers side by side in an oiled baking dish. Cover loosely with lightly oiled foil, tucking ends of foil into baking dish to prevent dripping during cooking. Bake 45 minutes.

# Marinated London Broil

*Sliced very thin, this dish can be served hot or at room temperature. Either way, the meat makes an excellent sandwich on any type of roll or crusty bread. You can also grill the meat on the barbecue.*

▶ *Yield: 4–6 servings*

| | |
|---|---|
| ½ | cup Parsley, Chive, and Garlic Rhine Wine (page 19) |
| ¼ | cup olive oil |
| 3 | cloves garlic, crushed |
| ½ | teaspoon freshly ground black pepper |
| 1 | London broil (2½–3 pounds) |

Blend wine, olive oil, garlic, and pepper thoroughly with a fork. Pour half the mixture into a large glass baking dish. Place meat in dish, and pour remaining marinade over. Cover with plastic wrap and let marinate for at least 6 hours in refrigerator, turning several times.

Remove meat from refrigerator 20 minutes before cooking. Preheat broiler. Place meat on broiler pan, and pour half the marinade over. Broil 10 to 15 minutes, or until browned. Turn, pour the remaining marinade over meat, and broil until browned. For medium to well done, continue to cook in 300°F oven until cooked as desired.

# Stuffed Marinated Flank Steak

*This dish can be made several hours before serving. Slice into 1½-inch pieces before reheating, loosely covered with foil, in a 250°F oven for 15 minutes.*

▶ *Yield: 4 servings*

| | |
|---|---|
| 1 | flank steak (1½–2 pounds), at least 1 inch thick |
| 1½ | cups Parsley and Savory Merlot (page 24) |
| ¼ | cup olive oil |
| 1 | teaspoon dry mustard |
| 2 | cloves garlic, crushed |
| ½ | teaspoon freshly ground black pepper |
| 1 | cup water |
| 1 | tablespoon butter or margarine |
| ½ | cup chopped onion |
| 1 | stalk celery, diced |
| 2½ | cups prepared stuffing mix |

With a sharp knife, cut a pocket in thickest side of flank steak, being careful not to cut through top or bottom of meat.

Mix ½ cup of the wine, olive oil, dry mustard, garlic, and pepper with a fork until thoroughly blended. Pour half the mixture into a large glass baking dish. Place meat on top of marinade, and pour the remaining marinade over meat. Cover with plastic wrap and refrigerate, marinating at least 2 hours on each side.

In a medium-size saucepan over medium heat, combine water and ½ cup of the wine. Melt butter in mixture. Stir in onion and celery, and cook about 10 minutes. Remove from heat and stir in stuffing mix. Let cool about 5 minutes.

Preheat oven to 350°F. Remove flank steak from marinade and fill pocket with stuffing. Place on a rack on a rimmed baking sheet. Pour about ¼ cup of marinade over flank steak. Cook in oven for 30 minutes. Reduce heat to 300°F, and cook meat an additional 10 minutes. Transfer to platter to cool for 5 minutes before slicing.

Deglaze baking sheet with remaining ½ cup wine. Pour over sliced flank steak, and serve.

# Burgundy Beef Stew

*Using top round steak in this dish reduces the cooking time.*

▶ *Yield: 4–6 servings*

|   |   |
|---|---|
| 1½ | pounds top round steak, cut into cubes |
| 4 | tablespoons olive oil |
| 1½ | cups Thyme and Marjoram Burgundy (page 23) |
| 1 | onion, chopped |
| 3 | carrots, peeled and sliced |
| 2 | large potatoes, peeled and cubed |
| 1 | package (10 ounces) frozen green beans, defrosted |
| 1 | tablespoon cornstarch |

In a large saucepan, brown meat in olive oil over medium heat. (Do not crowd.) Remove meat and set aside.

Reduce heat to low, and pour 1 cup of the wine into saucepan. Add onion, carrots, and potatoes. Simmer, covered, stirring occasionally, about 30 minutes, or until vegetables are tender. Add meat and the remaining ½ cup wine. Simmer, stirring often, an additional 30 minutes. Stir in green beans, cooking until heated through.

Remove ½ cup of liquid from saucepan and blend in cornstarch. Stir back into stew. Increase heat to medium, and simmer, stirring constantly, until gravy reaches desired consistency.

# Beef and Sun-Dried Tomatoes

*Prepare the tomatoes and beef in the morning, then cook and assemble later in the day. Serve warm or cold with crusty bread.*

▶ *Yield: 4 servings*

| | |
|---|---|
| 1½ | ounces sun-dried tomatoes |
| 1 | cup Sun-Dried Tomato and Garlic Merlot (page 25) |
| 4 | tablespoons olive oil |
| 2 | pounds top round steak, about 1½ inches thick |
| | red leaf lettuce |
| ½ | cup chopped scallions |

Cut tomatoes into ¼-inch strips. Place in a medium-size glass bowl. In a small bowl, mix wine and olive oil with a fork until well blended. Pour half the marinade over tomatoes. Set aside for at least 4 hours.

Place meat in a medium-size baking dish. Pour the remaining marinade over meat. Turn meat to coat both sides. Cover with plastic wrap and refrigerate at least 4 hours, turning once. Remove meat from refrigerator 30 minutes before cooking.

Preheat broiler. Place meat on broiler rack, broiling about 8 minutes on each side, or until cooked through. Let cool slightly before cutting into ¼-inch slices.

Line serving plates with lettuce leaves. Place several slices of meat on top of lettuce. Pour marinated sun-dried tomatoes over meat. Sprinkle with chopped scallions.

# Beef and Broccoli Stir-Fry

*This spicy dish is quick to make.*

▶ *Yield: 4 servings*

- 1½ pounds top round steak
- 1½ cups Thai Pepper Chardonnay (page 16)
- 1 tablespoon sesame seed oil
- 2 tablespoons canola oil
- ½ pound fresh broccoli florets, rinsed and drained
- 1 large onion, quartered
- 1 tablespoon sesame seeds
- 4 cups cooked rice

Cut steak into ¼-inch slices. Place in a medium-size glass baking dish. In a small bowl, combine ½ cup of the wine and sesame seed oil with a fork until well blended. Pour over sliced meat. Cover with plastic wrap and refrigerate at least 2 hours.

In a large skillet, combine another ½ cup of the wine and canola oil. Add broccoli, onion, and sesame seeds. Cook over high heat, stirring constantly, until vegetables are tender and liquid has evaporated, about 5 minutes. Transfer to a bowl. Place meat in skillet and cook, stirring constantly, until meat is browned. Reduce heat to medium and add vegetable mixture and remaining ½ cup of wine. Heat through, stirring until well blended. Serve over rice.

Sesame seed oil is extracted from roasted sesame seeds. A highly concentrated oil, it is used as a flavoring rather than as a cooking oil. Use sparingly in marinades and as a last-minute addition to season cooked foods.

## Pork Strips and Onion Pain Bagnet

*This dish can be prepared several hours ahead. Since each pork-and-onion-filled crusty roll is individually wrapped, it's great for a take-along lunch.*

▶ *Yield: 4 servings*

|       |                                          |
|-------|------------------------------------------|
| 1½    | cups Basil and Garlic Rosé (page 29)     |
| 2     | tablespoons olive oil                    |
| 1     | pound boneless pork, cut into ½-inch strips |
| 2     | tablespoons butter or margarine          |
| 2     | onions, sliced                           |
| 4–6   | fresh spinach leaves                     |
| 1     | roasted yellow pepper (page 50)          |
| 4     | crusty rolls                             |

In a small bowl, blend ½ cup of the wine and olive oil thoroughly with a fork. Place pork strips in a medium-size glass baking dish. Pour marinade over pork. Cover with plastic wrap. Refrigerate at least 2 hours, turning pork strips several times.

In a large skillet, melt 1 tablespoon of the butter with ½ cup of the wine. Add onions and cook over medium heat, stirring occasionally, until slightly golden brown. Transfer to platter.

Place pork strips in skillet and cook over medium heat until all sides are browned. Remove to platter. Let skillet cool for a few minutes. Slowly pour the remaining ½ cup of wine into the skillet and deglaze to make sauce. Stir in remaining 1 tablespoon of butter.

Split rolls. Pour ½ teaspoon of sauce on top and bottom inside of roll. Layer with spinach, pork strips, roasted yellow pepper, and onions. Close roll and wrap tightly in foil. Let sit at least 30 minutes before serving.

# Peppered Pork Steaks with Pinot Noir Sauce

*The pepper coating on the pork steaks is absorbed in the wine sauce, giving this dish a spicy touch.*

▶ *Yield: 2–4 servings*

> 1¼ cups Mustard and Garlic Pinot Noir (page 26)
> 4 tablespoons olive oil
> 2 cloves garlic, crushed
> 4 boneless pork steaks
> 2 teaspoons freshly ground black pepper
> 1 tablespoon butter or margarine

In a small bowl, mix ½ cup of the wine, 2 tablespoons of the olive oil, and the crushed garlic thoroughly with a fork. Place pork steaks in a medium-size glass baking dish. Pour marinade over, turning pork to coat. Cover with plastic wrap and refrigerate for at least 2 hours, turning once.

Transfer pork steaks to a platter and sprinkle both sides with pepper. In a large skillet over medium heat, blend the remaining 2 tablespoons of olive oil and ¼ cup of the wine. Sauté pork steaks until cooked through and browned on each side, about 20 minutes. Transfer to platter.

Slowly pour the remaining ½ cup of wine into skillet and deglaze to make sauce. Stir in butter. Pour sauce over pork steaks.

# Ham Steaks with Burgundy Honey Mustard Sauce

*Delicious and quick to make, these ham steaks can be served with eggs for a brunch or with mashed potatoes for dinner.*

▶ *Yield: 2–4 servings*

- 1 tablespoon butter or margarine
- 4 ham steaks, ½ inch thick
- ½ cup Thyme and Marjoram Burgundy (page 23)
- 1 tablespoon Dijon mustard
- 1 tablespoon honey

In a large skillet, melt butter over medium heat. Cook ham steaks, turning once, until browned on both sides. Remove to platter.

Reduce heat to low and slowly add wine to skillet. Stir in mustard and honey, cooking until well blended and liquid is slightly reduced. Increase heat to medium, return ham steaks to pan, and cook several minutes on each side. Place ham steaks on individual plates or serving platter, and pour sauce over.

# Chapter Twelve

# Seafood

*They say a fish should swim thrice —*
*first it should swim in the sea, then it should swim in butter*
*and at last, sirrah, it should swim in good claret.*

— Jonathan Swift

The seafood used in this chapter — shrimp, scallops, white fish fillets, and crabmeat — are mild in flavor. Since they are light in color, all the recipes here use varietals of white wine.

For dark fish, which require heartier marinades and sauces, use rosés and red wines. Try a Dill and Lemon Rosé with salmon, or a Chive and Garlic Cabernet Sauvignon with mackerel (see page 128). You can substitute just about any seafood and flavored wine combination in any of the seafood recipes here.

Most of these recipes are easy to prepare. There's a variety of cooking methods offered — sautéing, baking, broiling, and even microwaving.

# Shrimp Nachos

*The tangy marinated shrimp add a special touch to this popular dish.*

▶ *Yield: 4 servings*

1 pound (about 20) large raw shrimp, peeled and deveined
1 cup Cilantro, Lime, and Garlic Rhine Wine (page 19)
2 tablespoons olive oil
1 package (8–10 ounces) tortilla chips
1 jar (10–12 ounces) salsa
1 can (4 ounces) diced green chilies
8 ounces Monterey Jack cheese, shredded (2 cups)

## Variations

For dark-colored fish, try these recipes for flavored wines.

### Dill and Lemon Rosé

8 sprigs dill
½ lemon, cut into 2 pieces
2 cups rosé

Place dill and lemon in a 1-quart jar, pour wine over, and cover. Store in a cool, dim place for at least 2 weeks before testing flavor.

### Chive and Garlic Cabernet Sauvignon

1 cup snipped chives (2-inch pieces)
3 cloves garlic, peeled and cut in half lengthwise
2 cups Cabernet Sauvignon

Place chives and garlic in a 1-quart glass jar. Pour wine over and cover. Place in a cool, dim place for at least 2 weeks before testing flavor.

Place shrimp in a single layer in a glass baking dish. In a glass measuring cup, thoroughly mix ½ cup of the wine and 1 tablespoon of the olive oil with a fork. Pour over shrimp. Cover shrimp with plastic wrap, place in the refrigerator, and marinate at least 3 hours, turning several times.

In a large skillet over medium heat, blend the remaining ½ cup wine and 1 table-spoon of olive oil. Sauté shrimp until pink and just cooked through. Transfer to a platter.

Preheat oven to 375°F. Place half the tortilla chips on a baking sheet, slightly overlapping. Layer with half the salsa, all the shrimp, the chilies, and half the cheese. Top with remaining tortilla chips and salsa, and sprinkle with remaining cheese. Bake 15 minutes, or until cheese has melted and center is heated through.

# Breaded Shrimp

*Marinating the shrimp with a flavored wine and breading with flavored crumbs enhances this dish.*

▶ *Yield: 2–4 servings*

- 1 pound (about 20) large raw shrimp, peeled and deveined
- 1 cup Herb, Lemon, and Garlic Chablis Blanc (page 18)
- 1 large egg
- ½ cup unbleached all-purpose flour
- 1 cup flavored bread crumbs (page 38)
- canola oil

Place shrimp in a single layer in a glass baking dish. Pour ½ cup of the wine over, turning shrimp to coat. Cover with plastic wrap, place in refrigerator, and marinate at least 4 hours, turning several times.

In a pie plate, mix egg with the remaining ½ cup of wine until thoroughly blended. Coat shrimp with flour, dip into egg mixture, then cover with bread crumbs.

In a large skillet, fry shrimp in about ½ inch of canola oil over medium heat until golden brown. Drain on paper towels.

# Broiled Shrimp

*Quick and easy to prepare, yet special enough to serve to company.*

▶ *Yield: 4 servings*

- 1 pound (about 20) large raw shrimp, peeled and deveined, with tails left on
- 2 tablespoons butter or margarine
- ½ cup Chervil, Chive, and Dill Rhine Wine (page 20)
- ½ cup flavored bread crumbs (page 38)

Preheat broiler. Place shrimp in a single layer in a rimmed baking sheet.

In a small saucepan, melt butter with wine, stirring well to blend. Pour mixture evenly over shrimp, and sprinkle with bread crumbs. Cook under broiler about 10 minutes, or until bread crumbs are browned and shrimp is cooked through.

Divide among serving plates, and spoon sauce over each serving.

# Sautéed Scallop Puffs

*This filling can be baked in puff pastry shells or, for a lighter version, in natural baking shells. It can also be used as a filling for crepes.*

▶ *Yield: 3–4 servings*

> 1 pound scallops (bay or sea)
> 1 cup Rosemary and Garlic Chardonnay (page 14)
> 4–6 puff pastry bake-and-fill shells or natural baking shells
> 1 tablespoon butter or margarine
> 2 cloves garlic, crushed
> ½ cup finely diced onion
> 1 cup diced sweet red pepper
> 1 cup mayonnaise

Place scallops in a small glass baking dish. (If using sea scallops, cut scallops in half.) Pour ½ cup of the wine over. Cover scallops with plastic wrap, place in refrigerator, and marinate at least 2 hours, turning several times.

Prepare puff pastry shells according to package directions.

In a medium-size skillet over medium heat, melt butter with ¼ cup of the wine. Add garlic, onion, and red pepper. Cook, stirring often, until tender, about 10 minutes. Reduce heat to low. Stir in scallops and marinade, cover, and cook about 5 minutes, or until scallops are cooked through.

In a small bowl, blend the remaining ¼ cup of wine with the mayonnaise. Stir into scallop mixture, blending well. Cook until heated through.

Preheat broiler. Fill prepared puff pastry shells (or natural baking shells), dividing mixture evenly among the shells. Place under broiler and cook until golden brown.

# Scallop Cakes

*These scallop cakes are delicious either baked or sautéed.*

▶ *Yield: 12 scallop cakes*

|      |                                                      |
|------|------------------------------------------------------|
| 1    | pound scallops                                       |
| 1½   | cups Parsley and Garlic Chablis Blanc (page 16)      |
| 1    | tablespoon butter or margarine                       |
| 1    | small onion, chopped fine                            |
| 3    | cups coarse bread crumbs                             |
| ½    | cup chopped scallions                                |
| ½    | cup diced sweet red pepper                           |
| 2    | tablespoons fresh parsley                            |
| 1    | teaspoon Dijon mustard                               |
| ⅓    | cup mayonnaise                                        |
|      | butter or margarine for baking or sautéing           |

Place scallops in a small glass baking dish. Pour ½ cup of the wine over. Cover with plastic wrap, place in refrigerator, and marinate at least 2 hours, turning several times.

In a medium-size skillet, sauté scallops with marinade over medium heat until just cooked through. Cool slightly, drain, and chop. In the same skillet, melt butter over low heat. Sauté onion until tender. Cool.

Place bread crumbs in a medium-size glass bowl. Pour remaining cup of wine over, tossing quickly to moisten crumbs. Add onion, scallions, red pepper, and parsley, mixing well. Stir in scallops. In a small bowl, blend mustard and mayonnaise together. Stir into scallop mixture.

If planning to bake, preheat oven to 450°F. Form ¼-cup scoops into patties. Place on a greased baking sheet, dot each patty with butter, and bake until golden brown on both sides, about 10 minutes.

To sauté, cook patties in butter over medium heat until golden brown on both sides.

# Fish Fillets with Caramelized Onion Wine Sauce

*Fish fillets, caramelized onions, and roasted red peppers combine to form this tasty and attractive dish cooked in the microwave.*

▶ *Yield: 4 servings*

> 1   pound flounder, cod, pollack, or any other white fish fillets
>     freshly ground black pepper
> 3   tablespoons butter or margarine
> 1   cup Coriander and Peppercorn Rhine Wine (page 20)
> 3   Vidalia onions, sliced
> 1   roasted red pepper, cut into ½-inch strips (page 50)

Place fillets in a medium-size glass baking dish. Sprinkle with pepper to taste. Set aside.

In a medium-size skillet over low heat, melt 2 tablespoons of the butter with ¼ cup of the wine. Add onions, cover, and cook about 10 minutes, or until tender, stirring occasionally. Increase heat to high, add an additional ¼ cup of the wine, and cook, stirring constantly, until onions are golden brown. Spread onions over fillets. Crisscross pepper strips over onions.

Slowly pour the remaining ½ cup of wine into skillet and deglaze to make sauce. Add the remaining 1 tablespoon of butter. Pour sauce over fillets.

Cover loosely with wax paper. Cook at high in the microwave, turning once during cooking, until fish flakes easily with a fork, about 8 minutes. Let sit, covered, for 2 minutes before serving.

# Herbal Lemon Stuffed Fillets

*Using slices of fresh lemon adds color and a tangy flavor. Cooking in the microwave keeps the fish moist.*

▶ *Yield: 4–6 servings*

| | |
|---|---|
| 1 | pound white fish fillets |
| 4 | tablespoons butter or margarine |
| 1 | cup Herb, Lemon, and Garlic Chablis Blanc (page 18) |
| 1 | lemon, sliced thin |
| 2 | stalks celery, chopped fine |
| 1 | small onion, chopped |
| 16 | ounces fresh bread cubes |
| 2 | tablespoons fresh parsley, chopped (optional) |

Place fish fillets in a medium-size glass baking dish. Set aside.

In a large skillet over medium heat, melt butter with ½ cup of the wine. Add half of the lemon slices and cook about 5 minutes. Add celery and onion, and cook, stirring occasionally, about 10 minutes, or until celery and onion are tender. Remove and discard lemon slices.

Add bread cubes to pan, tossing quickly to coat pieces and mixing well with vegetable mixture. Spoon stuffing mixture over fillets in baking dish, and top with remaining lemon slices.

Slowly pour the remaining ½ cup of wine into the same skillet and deglaze to make sauce. Pour sauce over fillets. Cover loosely with wax paper. Cook at medium-high in microwave for 10 minutes, turning once. Fish will flake easily with a fork when cooked through. Top with fresh parsley, if desired.

Fresh bread cubes are easy to prepare from unsliced bread. Just cut the bread into ¾-inch-thick slices, stack three or four slices, and cut again, this time into ¾-inch squares. Try flavored breads and whole-grain breads for a variety of stuffings.

# Oven-Baked Fish Fillets

*A tasty lower-fat version of fried fish.*

▶ *Yield: 2–4 servings*

> 1 pound white fish fillets
> ½ cup Parsley, Chive, and Lemon Rhine Wine (page 20)
> 1 cup flavored bread crumbs (page 38)
> canola oil

Place fillets in a medium-size glass baking dish. Pour wine over, cover with plastic wrap, and marinate in refrigerator for at least 4 hours.

Preheat oven to 400°F. Coat fish fillets with bread crumbs. Cover bottom of baking sheet with oil and heat pan in oven until oil sizzles. Place fillets on hot baking sheet and cook about 10 minutes, or until golden brown. Turn to brown other side, adding more oil, if necessary. Drain on paper towels.

# Breaded Scallops with Basil and Garlic Mayonnaise

*Basil and Garlic Mayonnaise accentuates the flavor of the scallops.*

▶ *Yield: 2–4 servings*

> 1 pound sea scallops, rinsed
> ½ cup plus 2 tablespoons Basil and Garlic Chablis Blanc (page 17)
> 1 egg
> ½ cup unbleached all-purpose flour
> 1 cup bread crumbs
> canola oil
> 1 cup mayonnaise
> ¼ cup chopped fresh basil

Place scallops in a small baking dish. Pour ¼ cup of the wine over scallops and cover with plastic wrap. Marinate in refrigerator at least 2 hours.

In a pie plate, mix egg with ¼ cup of the wine. Coat scallops with flour, dip into egg mixture, then cover with bread crumbs. Pour 1 inch canola oil in a 4-quart pot. Over medium heat, cook oil until heated through. Add scallops and fry until golden brown on both sides. Drain on paper towels.

### Basil and Garlic Mayonnaise

In a small bowl, stir mayonnaise with remaining 2 tablespoons of wine until well blended. Stir in fresh basil.

# Seafood Crepes

*This delicate, flavorful filling can be made ahead. To reheat, cover with wax paper and cook at medium in microwave for 4 to 5 minutes, stirring once.*

▶ *Yield: 4 servings*

| | |
|---|---|
| 1 | pound (about 25) medium shrimp, peeled, deveined, and rinsed |
| 1/2 | pound scallops, rinsed |
| 1 | cup Lemon Dill Rhine Wine (page 19) |
| 1 | tablespoon butter or margarine |
| 2 | tablespoons unbleached all-purpose flour |
| 1/4 | cup grated Parmesan |
| | white pepper |
| 1 | can (6–8 ounces) crabmeat, drained |
| 6–8 | prepared crepes, at room temperature |

Place shrimp and scallops in a medium-size baking dish. Pour ¼ cup of the wine over. Cover with plastic wrap and marinate in refrigerator for at least 2 hours.

In a large skillet, melt butter with ¼ cup of the wine over medium heat. Sauté scallops and shrimp in wine mixture, stirring occasionally, until cooked through, about 5 minutes. Remove seafood with a slotted spoon to a dish. Reduce heat to low, slowly add flour to cooking liquid, stirring with a fork until well blended. Stir in remaining ½ cup of wine, Parmesan cheese, and white pepper. Add shrimp, scallops, and crabmeat. Mix thoroughly, cooking until seafood is heated through. Spoon into prepared crepes.

# Chapter Thirteen

# Desserts

*A wilderness of sweets...*

— John Milton *(Paradise Lost)*

A dessert crowns the meal. Raspberry Merlot Chocolate Mousse Cake, Spiced Nectarine Tart, Rice Custard, Strawberry Rosé Parfait, and Hazelnut Gâteau are just some of the recipes in this chapter. When planning desserts, include them as part of the entire meal, keeping in mind the ingredients used for the first course, entrées, and side dishes. See Chapter Six, "Menus for Entertaining," on page 39 for some suggestions.

For low-fat desserts, fruit marinated in flavored wines is especially enjoyable. Depending on the fruit and wine used, the fruit can be marinated for a few hours, or overnight. Check every few hours for the fruit's saturation point. If the fruit has absorbed too much of the flavored wine, puree and use as a filling for cakes or as a spread on breads and muffins.

# Strawberry Rosé Parfait

*This wine-flavored custard is layered with marinated pureed strawberries and crushed cappuccino or hazelnut cookie crumbs in a pretty stemmed glass to form a delicious and attractive dessert. Make several hours ahead of serving.*

▶ *Yield: 2 servings*

- 4 large egg yolks
- 4 tablespoons sugar
- ½ cup Strawberry Rosé (page 31)
- ⅓ cup crushed cappuccino or hazelnut cookie crumbs
- 1 cup marinated strawberries from Strawberry Rosé, strained and pureed

In the top of a 1-quart double boiler, or in a 1-quart glass bowl placed over a pan of simmering water, mix egg yolks and sugar with a wooden spoon until well blended. Slowly stir wine into egg mixture, scraping sides of bowl often, until mixture coats spoon, about 15 minutes. Remove from heat. Let mixture cool, stirring occasionally, until completely cool.

Spoon 1 tablespoon of the cookie crumbs into each clear parfait glass. Top with a small amount of pureed strawberries, and then with custard. Repeat alternating layers, ending with the custard. Sprinkle with cookie crumbs. Cover with plastic wrap and chill in refrigerator until ready to serve.

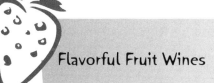

## Flavorful Fruit Wines

Make flavored fruit and spice wines to drink. Add about 2 cups of fruit to 1 quart of wine. Add a touch of nutmeg, cinnamon, or clove, if desired. Let sit, refrigerated, for at least 3 weeks before testing. The fruit can be removed and used, pureed, for filling and spreads, or left in the wine to be enjoyed.

# Rice Custard with Fruit Topping

*The secret to this deliciously flavored rice is in the cooking. You can use precooked rice, but it will not have the same subtle orange flavor.*

▶ *Yield: 6–8 servings*

### Rice Custard

1½   cups Orange Mango Chardonnay (page 13)
1   cup half-and-half
1   cup sugar
2   cups instant long-grain rice
1½   cups water
2   large eggs

### Fruit Topping

1   orange, peeled, cut into sections, and diced
1   mango, peeled and chopped
3   kiwi, peeled and diced

**To make rice custard:** In a medium-size saucepan over medium heat, bring wine, ½ cup of the half-and-half, and ½ cup of the sugar to a boil, stirring constantly. Stir in rice. Remove from heat, cover, and let sit 10 minutes. Stir well, and let sit an additional 5 minutes. Transfer to a glass bowl, cover with plastic wrap, and store in refrigerator until ready to use. Rice can be made up to 1 day ahead.

In a large saucepan over medium heat, mix water and remaining ½ cup of half-and-half. Add remaining ½ cup of sugar, stirring to dissolve. Add rice and cook, stirring occasionally, until mixture comes to a boil. Reduce heat to low. Cook, stirring frequently, until mixture is slightly thick and creamy.

In a small bowl, beat eggs with a whisk until thoroughly blended. Stir 1 cup of the rice mixture into beaten eggs and mix well. Pour back into saucepan and continue to cook over low heat, stirring, until mixture has thickened, about 5 minutes. Cool completely.

**To make fruit topping:** Gently mix orange, mango, and kiwi in a small glass bowl until just blended. When ready to serve, spoon custard into individual serving bowls and top with fruit.

# Spiced Nectarine Tart

*This tart can be made with any combination of fruit and flavored wine. Try peaches or plums instead of nectarines. Or use the Raspberry Chardonnay with marinated raspberries.*

▶ *Yield: 8 servings*

| | |
|---|---|
| 1½ | pounds (about 6) nectarines |
| ½ | cup Spiced Cinnamon Pinot Noir (page 26) |
| | pastry crust to fit a 10-inch tart pan with removable bottom |
| ⅓ | cup sugar |
| 2 | tablespoons unbleached all-purpose flour |
| 1 | tablespoon cornstarch |
| 2 | large egg yolks |
| ⅔ | cup half-and-half |
| ⅔ | cup water |
| ½ | teaspoon vanilla |

Cut nectarines in half, remove pits, and slice fruit thin. Place in a single layer in a medium-size glass baking dish. Pour wine over. Cover with plastic wrap and marinate in refrigerator at least 2 hours.

Preheat oven to 375°F. Roll or pat pastry crust to fit tart pan. Bake 15 minutes, or until golden brown and set. Let cool.

In a medium-size saucepan, combine sugar, flour, and cornstarch. In a small glass bowl, whisk eggs, half-and-half, and water until well blended. Whisk into flour mixture in saucepan. Cook over medium heat, stirring often with a wooden spoon, until mixture thickens and coats spoon, about 15 minutes. Whisk in vanilla. Cool until custard forms soft mounds.

Spoon custard into prepared pastry crust. Drain nectarines well and arrange on top of custard. Refrigerate until ready to serve.

# Fruit in Spiced Wine Syrup

*The syrup in this dessert requires a day to thicken, so plan to prepare it ahead of time. Also excellent as a topping for pancakes, waffles, and ice cream, the syrup will keep for at least a week in the refrigerator.*

▶ *Yield: 4 servings; makes about ¾ cup syrup*

> 1  cup Spiced Cinnamon Pinot Noir (page 26)
> 8  tablespoons sugar
> 1  pound ripe peaches, nectarines, or plums, or any combination

Blend wine and sugar in a small saucepan over medium heat. Bring to a boil and cook, stirring constantly, 5 minutes. Let cool. Transfer to a small glass bowl, cover with plastic wrap, and store in refrigerator overnight.

When ready to serve, cut fruit into pieces. Place fruit in individual serving bowls or plates, and spoon syrup over.

For softer fruit, place cut fruit in a single layer in a small glass baking dish and pour syrup over. Cover with plastic wrap and refrigerate at least 2 hours or up to 8 hours.

# Nectarine and Mixed Berry Sorbet

*This refreshing sorbet can be made a day ahead. Simply puree about an hour before serving.*

▶ *Yield: 6–8 servings*

> 1  pound nectarines, peeled and cut into 1-inch pieces
> 1  package (12 ounces) frozen unsweetened mixed berries
> ¾  cup Raspberry Merlot (page 25)
> ½  cup sugar

In a large saucepan over high heat, bring nectarines, berries, and wine to a boil. Reduce heat to low, simmer, partially covered and stirring occasionally with a wooden spoon, until nectarines are tender, about 10 minutes. Stir in sugar until dissolved. Let cool.

Puree fruit mixture in food processor until smooth. Pour into a small freezer-proof ceramic casserole dish. Cover loosely with wax paper. Freeze until firm, about 1 hour. Puree in food processor a second time. Return to freezer, and remove 10 minutes before serving time.

# Hazelnut Gâteau

*A moist, rich torte with a slightly crunchy texture, this dessert can be prepared several days ahead of serving.*

▶ *Yield: 12–16 servings*

| | |
|---|---|
| ¼ | pound (1 stick) butter or margarine, softened |
| 1½ | cups sugar |
| 4 | eggs |
| ½ | cup Spiced Cinnamon Pinot Noir (page 26) |
| 1 | cup unbleached all-purpose flour |
| 1½ | cups finely chopped hazelnuts |

Butter an 8-inch cake pan, line with parchment paper, and butter again.

Preheat oven to 325°F. In a medium-size mixing bowl, cream butter with sugar. Add eggs, one at a time, beating well after each addition. Stir in wine, flour, and hazelnuts, mixing thoroughly. Pour into prepared pan and bake 45 minutes, or until a tester inserted in the center comes out clean.

While warm, gently loosen edges of gâteau with a sharp knife. Cool in pan. Unmold onto wire rack, peel off parchment paper, and invert onto serving plate. Cut into thin slices.

Hazelnuts are also known as filberts. If they are not available, substitute walnuts.

# Raspberry Merlot Chocolate Mousse Cake

*Cut this very rich and dense cake into thin slices and top with fresh whipped cream.*

▶ *Yield: 12–16 servings*

| | |
|---|---|
| ⅓ | cup plus 1 tablespoon Raspberry Merlot (page 25) |
| ⅓ | cup marinated raspberries from Raspberry Merlot, strained and pureed |
| ¾ | cup sugar |
| ¼ | pound (1 stick) butter, cut into 4 pieces |
| 12 | ounces semisweet chocolate chips |
| 4 | large eggs |
| | whipped cream (optional) |

Grease an 8-inch round cake pan, line with parchment paper, and grease again.

In a medium-size saucepan, combine ⅓ cup of the wine with marinated raspberries and sugar. Cook over medium heat, stirring occasionally with a wooden spoon, until mixture starts to boil. Stir in butter until melted and mixture starts to boil again. Remove from heat, and stir in chocolate chips until thoroughly blended. Add additional tablespoon of wine.

Preheat oven to 350°F. Whisk eggs in a medium-size mixing bowl until well blended. Slowly stir into chocolate mixture, mixing well. Pour into prepared pan.

Bake for 30 minutes, reduce heat to 300°F, and bake an additional 10 minutes. Top of cake will be slightly dry. Cool on wire rack about 1 hour, then loosen edges with a sharp knife. Invert onto serving plate, and peel off parchment paper. Cake will be very moist. Cover loosely with wax paper and refrigerate until ready to serve. Serve topped with whipped cream, if desired.

# Peach and Almond Cobbler

*For a more pronounced wine flavor, this dish can be made several days ahead and reheated in the microwave. Serve warm with vanilla ice cream or frozen yogurt.*

▶ *Yield: 4–6 servings*

| | |
|---|---|
| 1 | cup unbleached all-purpose flour |
| 1 | cup sugar |
| 2 | teaspoons baking powder |
| ³⁄₄ | cup Peach Chablis Blanc (page 18) |
| 3 | tablespoons cornstarch |
| 2 | cups marinated peaches from Peach Chablis Blanc |
| 4 | tablespoons butter or margarine |
| ½ | cup half-and-half |
| ½ | cup sliced almonds |

In a medium-size glass bowl, blend flour, ½ cup of the sugar, and baking powder with a fork. Set aside. Preheat oven to 400°F.

In a medium-size saucepan over low heat, combine wine with cornstarch, stirring with a wooden spoon, until well blended. Add remaining ½ cup of sugar and marinated peaches. Bring to a boil, stirring occasionally. While peach mixture is cooking, cut butter into flour mixture with a pastry blender. Stir in half-in-half, forming a soft dough.

Pour peaches into a medium-size baking dish. Sprinkle with all but 1 table-spoon of almonds. Spoon dough over, and top with the remaining almonds. Bake 30 minutes.

# Orange Tea Loaf

*A moist, dense loaf with a subtle orange flavor.*

▶ *Yield: 8–10 servings*

|       |                                              |
|-------|----------------------------------------------|
| ¼     | pound (1 stick) butter or margarine          |
| 1     | cup sugar                                    |
| 2     | eggs                                         |
|       | grated rind of 1 orange                      |
| ¼     | cup juice from orange in Orange Rhine Wine   |
| ¼     | cup Orange Rhine Wine (page 21)              |
| 1     | tablespoon frozen orange juice concentrate   |
| 1     | cup sour cream                               |
| 2     | cups unbleached all-purpose flour            |
| 2     | teaspoons baking powder                      |
| 2     | teaspoons baking soda                        |
| 1     | cup pecans                                   |

Preheat oven to 300°F. Grease a loaf pan.

In a large mixing bowl, cream butter with sugar. Slightly beat eggs in a medium-size glass bowl. Add orange rind, juice from orange in wine mixture, wine, orange juice concentrate, and sour cream. Stir with a fork until well blended. Add to creamed mixture and blend well.

Stir in flour, baking powder, and baking soda until well blended. Add pecans. Pour into loaf pan. Bake 1 hour, or until set in center. Let cool in loaf pan for 10 minutes before inverting onto cooling rack. Cool completely before slicing.

# Chocolate Raspberry Pudding or Mousse

*This rich, dense chocolate pudding can easily be turned into a lighter version of Chocolate Raspberry Mousse. Both are delicious.*

▶ *Yield: 4–6 servings*

| | |
|---|---|
| ½ | cup unsweetened cocoa |
| ¾ | cup sugar |
| ¼ | cup cornstarch |
| 1½ | cups half-and-half |
| 1½ | cups Raspberry Cabernet Sauvignon (page 27) |
| 1 | cup heavy cream (for mousse) |

Combine cocoa, sugar, and cornstarch in a medium-size saucepan, stirring until well blended. In a 1-quart container with a spout, mix half-and-half with wine. Slowly stir into chocolate mixture. Cook over low heat, stirring constantly, until mixture thickens, about 20 minutes. (Do not let mixture boil.)

For pudding, pour into dessert dishes. Cover with wax paper, let cool, then refrigerate, covering each dish with plastic wrap.

For mousse, transfer pudding to a bowl, cover with wax paper, and let cool. In a medium-size glass bowl, beat heavy cream until stiff peaks form. With a wooden spoon, fold into pudding. Place in dessert dishes, cover with plastic wrap, and refrigerate until ready to serve.

This version of mousse does not use raw eggs, thereby dispelling any concerns you might have about cooking with them. Instead, whipped heavy cream provides the light, creamy texture.

# Black Forest Cherry Cake

*Plan to serve this cake on the same day it is made. Leftovers will last an extra day or two if tightly wrapped when stored in the refrigerator.*

▶ *Yield: 12–16 servings*

### Whipped-Cream Cake

- 2 cups unbleached all-purpose flour
- 1½ cups sugar
- 1 tablespoon baking powder
- 3 eggs
- 2 teaspoons vanilla
- 2 cups heavy cream

### Cherry Filling

- ¼ cup sugar
- 1 tablespoon cornstarch
- 1 cup Sweet Cherry Cabernet Sauvignon (page 27)
  marinated cherries from Sweet Cherry Cabernet Sauvignon, drained and coarsely chopped

### Whipped-Cream Frosting

- 1½ cups heavy cream
- ¼ cup confectioners' sugar
  unsweetened cocoa

Preheat oven to 325°F. Line two 9-inch round cake pans with parchment paper. Grease paper.

**To make cake:** In a large mixing bowl, blend flour, sugar, and baking powder. In a small bowl, lightly beat eggs with vanilla. With mixer running, add egg mixture to flour mixture, blending until all flour is incorporated.

In a medium-size glass bowl, beat 2 cups of heavy cream until stiff peaks form. With a wooden spoon, fold heavy cream into batter. Blend well. Spread into parchment-lined pans. Bake 30 minutes, or until firm in center. Cool in pan 10 minutes before inverting onto cooling rack. Remove parchment while cake is warm. Cool completely.

**To make cherry filling:** In a small saucepan, mix sugar with cornstarch. Slowly stir in wine. Bring to a boil over medium-high heat. Add cherries. Bring to a second boil, and cook 3 minutes, stirring constantly. Remove from heat; let cool completely.

**To make frosting:** With a mixer, beat 1½ cups of heavy cream and confectioners' sugar in a medium-size bowl until stiff peaks form.

**To assemble cake:** Place one cake layer, bottom side up, on serving plate. Spoon ½-inch rim of whipped-cream frosting around outer edge of layer. Fill with cherry filling. Place in refrigerator about 1 hour for filling to jell. (Place remaining frosting in refrigerator, covered with plastic wrap, until ready to frost cake.) Invert second layer on top. Top with remaining frosting, and sprinkle with unsweetened cocoa.

# Index

Sun-Dried Tomato and Roasted Garlic Dip, 57
Sun-Dried Tomato and Spinach Tart, 55
Sun-Dried Tomato Cheese Torta, 54
Sun-Dried Tomatoes, 25, 38, 53
Sun-Dried Tomato Pastry Swirls, 53
Sweet Cherry Cabernet Sauvignon, 27
Syrup, spiced wine, 140

## T

Tarts
    nectarine, 139
    onion and zucchini, 95
    tomato and spinach 55
Thai Pepper Chardonnay, 16
Three-Bean Chili, 91
Thyme and Marjoram Burgundy, 23
Thyme, Tarragon, and Chive Cabernet
    Sauvignon, 26, 68
Timbales, spinach, 106
Tomato and onion relish, 82
Tomato and Shrimp Gaspacho, 62
Tomatoes, sun-dried, 38, 53
Tomato sauce, 79

Torta, tomato and cheese, 54
Torte, hazelnut, 141

## V

Vegetable Pot Pie, 100
Vegetable Soup, 65
Vegetable-Stuffed Eggplant, 101

## W

Wine, 5, 74
    fruit, 18, 21, 25, 27, 31, 137
    red, 6
    rosé, 6
    white, 5–6
Wine, flavored
    making, 7, 9, 10–11, 137
    red, 22–27, 128
    rosé, 28–31, 128
    storing, 8
    using, 8, 36, 67
    white, 12–21
Wine sauce, 79
Whipped-Cream Frosting, 146
White Bean Dip, 58

# Other Storey Titles You Will Enjoy

**Country Wines: Making & Using Wines from Herbs, Fruits, Flowers & More,** by Pattie Vargas and Rich Gulling. How to make delicious wines from fruits and berries, flowers, and herbs. 176 pages. Paperback. US $12.95 / CAN $18.50. Order #0-88266-749-1.

**From Vines to Wines: The Complete Guide to Growing Grapes and Making Your Own Wine,** by Jeff Cox. Cox takes the home winemaker through the entire process from evaluating the site and choosing the best grape species, to vineyard care, bottling, supplies, and troubleshooting. 288 pages. Paperback. US $14.95 / CAN $21.50. Order #0-88266-528-6.

**The Herbal Palate Cookbook,** by Maggie Oster & Sal Gilbertie. Through more than 130 recipes, this book creates an innovative palate for fresh herbs. From appetizers to desserts, each recipe offers informative information on the herbs used, as well as teaching readers how to cultivate herbs in small spaces and containers for fresh herbs year-round. 176 pages. Hardcover. US $29.95 / CAN $42.50. Order #0-88266-915-X.

**Herbal Vinegar,** by Maggie Oster. This book provides dozens of ideas for making and flavoring inexpensive and easy herb, spice, vegetable, and flower vinegars, as well as over 100 recipes for using flavored vinegars, instructions for growing herbs inside and out, and more than 100 vinegar-based personal and household uses and hints. 176 pages. Paperback. US $12.95 / CAN $18.50. Order #0-88266-843-9. Hardcover. US $18.95 / CAN $26.95. Order #0-88266-876-5.

**The Herb Gardener: A Guide for All Seasons,** by Susan McClure. McClure provides complete instructions on every conceivable aspect of herbs in the home and garden and helps the reader to successfully grow and use 75 different herbs throughout the year. 240 pages. Paperback. US $19.95 / CAN $28.50. Order #0-88266-873-0.

**Herb Mixtures & Spicy Blends,** edited by Deborah Balmuth. An essential guide to dozens of easy-to-make recipes that use herb mixtures and spice blends to create healthy, tasty dishes without a lot of added salt or fat. Also gives instructions for drying and storing, and time-saving tips for bottling and labeling. 160 pages. Paperback. US $12.95 / CAN $18.50. Order #0-88266-918-4. Hardcover. US $19.95 / CAN $28.50. Order #0-88266-919-2.

**Mustards, Ketchups & Vinegars,** by Carol W. Costenbader. Use the fruits and vegetables of the season to create a veritable cornucopia of the freshest condiments for your pantry and refrigerator, or for gift giving. 96 pages. Hardcover. US $16.95 / CAN $23.95. Order #0-88266-813-7.

These books and other Storey books are available at your bookstore, farm store, garden center, or directly from Storey Publishing, Schoolhouse Road, Pownal, Vermont 05261, or by calling 1-800-441-5700. www.storey.com